Great Escapes
South America

Photos by Tuca Reinés *Edited by* Angelika Taschen *Texts by* Christiane Reiter

Great Escapes
South America

TASCHEN

Contents Inhalt Sommaire

Price categories:		Preiskategorien:		Catégories de prix :	
$	up to 150 US$	$	bis 150 US$	$	jusqu'à 150 US$
$$	up to 250 US$	$$	bis 250 US$	$$	jusqu'à 250 US$
$$$	up to 450 US$	$$$	bis 450 US$	$$$	jusqu'à 450 US$
$$$$	over 450 US$	$$$$	über 450 US$	$$$$	plus de 450 US$

The play of light...
Pousada Maravilha, Fernando de Noronha

Pousada Maravilha,
Fernando de Noronha

The play of light

When Portuguese merchant Fernando de Noronha discovered the 21-island archipelago off the north-eastern coast of Brazil in 1503, he took little interest in it – after a cursory inspection of the bizarre formations of volcanic rock, he took to the ocean again, looking for greater adventures. Others who followed him stayed longer, though not always of their own free will – in the 18th century the main island was made a penal colony, and around 1930 a gaol for political prisoners was established. In the Second World War it was an air base, and in the 1960s a NASA satellite observation post. Tourism did not take off till Fernando de Noronha was declared a nature reserve in 1988. Since then, it has earned a name as one of Brazil's best diving areas, celebrated for its dolphins and turtles in particular. Those who aren't so interested in the underwater world, but are happy to enjoy a unique experience on dry land, will relish a stay at the Pousada Maravilha. The eight bungalows blend in naturally with their setting by a magical bay – the wood replicates the hues of the rocks, the pool picks up the blue of the sky and the ocean. Relax on cream futons or gently swaying hammocks. The occasional strong notes of colour – cushions or crockery – are the only added extras the design permits itself; otherwise, a purist tone is dominant, showing in the most appealing of ways just how well the simple life and luxury can go together.

Book to pack: "The Lizard's Smile" by João Ubaldo Ribeiro

Pousada Maravilha

BR 363, s/n – Sueste
Fernando de Noronha, PE
Brazil
CEP 53990 000
Tel: + 55 (81) 3619 0028
Fax: + 55 (81) 3619 0162
E-mail: reservas@pousadamaravilha.com.br
Website: www.pousadamaravilha.com.br

DIRECTIONS	350 km/225 miles off the north-east coast of Brazil, with daily flights from Natal and Recife
RATES	$$$$
ROOMS	5 bungalows for 2 people, 3 apartments for 4 people max.
FOOD	A delightful restaurant serving Mediterranean specialities. Room service is available
HISTORY	The first luxury hideaway on Fernando de Noronha
X-FACTOR	Purist design hotel affording plenty of privacy

Lichterspiele

Als der portugiesische Kaufmann Fernando de Noronha den Archipel mit 21 Inseln vor der Nordostküste Brasiliens 1503 entdeckte, interessierte er ihn kaum – nach wenigen Blicken auf das bizarr geformte Vulkangestein stach er wieder in See und segelte vermeintlich größeren Abenteuern entgegen. Andere, die nach ihm kamen, hielten es länger aus – wenn auch nicht immer ganz freiwillig: Im 18. Jahrhundert wurde die Hauptinsel zur Strafkolonie, um 1930 richtete man hier ein politisches Gefängnis ein. Im Zweiten Weltkrieg diente sie als Luftwaffenstützpunkt und in den 1960er-Jahren als Satellitenbeobachtungsposten der NASA. Der Tourismus begann erst, als Fernando de Noronha 1988 zum Naturschutzgebiet erklärt wurde – seitdem gilt der Archipel als eines der besten Tauchreviere Brasiliens und ist vor allem für seine Delfine und Meeresschildkröten berühmt. Wer sich nicht nur für die Unterwasserwelt interessiert, sondern auch an Land Einzigartiges erleben möchte, zieht am besten in die Pousada Maravilha. An einer zauberhaften Bucht passen sich die acht Bungalows wie selbstverständlich ihrer Umgebung an – das Holz nimmt den Farbton der Felsen auf, der Pool scheint direkt ins Blau von Himmel und Meer zu fließen, man entspannt auf cremefarbenen Futons oder in sanft schwingenden Hängematten. Ein paar Farbtupfer – Kissen oder Geschirr – sind die einzigen Extras, die sich das Design gönnt; ansonsten dominiert hier der Purismus und zeigt auf angenehmste Weise, wie gut *simple life* und Luxus zusammenpassen können.

Buchtipp: »Das Lächeln der Eidechse« von João Ubaldo Ribeiro

Jeux de lumière

Lorsque le marchand portugais Fernando de Noronha a découvert en 1503 cet archipel qui fait face à la côte nord-est du Brésil, on ne peut pas dire que les 21 îles l'aient captivé. Après avoir jeté quelques coups d'œil sur les roches volcaniques aux formes bizarres, il leva l'ancre et s'en alla vers de nouvelles aventures. D'autres sont venus après lui, mais ceux-là sont restés plus longtemps, et pas toujours de leur plein gré : au XVIIIe siècle, en effet, l'île principale devint un pénitencier, en 1930 on y construisit une prison politique. Au cours de la Deuxième Guerre mondiale, elle a servi de base aérienne et dans les années 1960, la N.A.S.A. y a installé un poste d'observation de satellites. Et puis Fernando de Norhona a été déclaré site naturel protégé, et le tourisme a fait son apparition. Aujourd'hui, l'endroit est considéré comme l'une des meilleures zones de plongée du Brésil et il est renommé pour ses dauphins et ses tortues de mer. La Pousada Maravilha est faite pour ceux qui non seulement s'intéressent au monde sous-marin mais aussi aux richesses uniques de la terre ferme. Les huit bungalows s'harmonisent tout naturellement avec le paysage de la baie superbe qui les entoure – le bois prend la couleur des rochers, la piscine semble couler dans le bleu du ciel et de la mer ; les futons couleur crème et les hamacs qui oscillent doucement sont propices à la détente. Les quelques accents de couleur des coussins et de la vaisselle sont les seuls « manquements » au design délibérément puriste qui montre avec beaucoup de charme combien la simplicité et le luxe font bon ménage.

Livre à emporter : « Le sourire du lézard » de João Ubaldo Ribeiro

ANREISE	350 Kilometer vor Brasiliens Nordostküste gelegen, tägliche Flüge ab Natal und Recife
PREIS	$$$$
ZIMMER	5 Bungalows für 2 Personen, 3 Apartments für maximal 4 Personen
KÜCHE	Schönes Restaurant mit mediterranen Spezialitäten, Zimmerservice möglich
GESCHICHTE	Das erste Luxus-Hideaway auf Fernando de Noronha
X-FAKTOR	Puristisches Designhotel mit viel Privatsphäre

ACCÈS	Situé à 350 kilomètres de la côte nord-est du Brésil, vols journaliers à partir de Natal et Recife
PRIX	$$$$
CHAMBRES	5 bungalows pour 2 personnes, 3 appartements pour 4 personnes maximum
RESTAURATION	Le beau restaurant offre des spécialités méditerranéennes, service de chambre possible
HISTOIRE	Le premier « refuge » de luxe sur Fernando de Noronha
LES « PLUS »	Le goût de la simplicité et beaucoup d'intimité

In the Garden of Eden...
Txai Resort, Bahia

Txai Resort, Bahia

In the Garden of Eden

Itacaré is in the south of Bahia, on the Cocoa Coast. In the mid-19th century, the "black gold" made it famous, and it became the foremost port of export in the region. Brazil's great writer Jorge Amado immortalised that cocoa boom in his novel "Gabriela, Clove and Cinnamon" – Amado was born in the region himself, on a cocoa plantation near Ilhéus. But ever since 1989 a fungal blight has annually been wiping out almost the entire crop all along the entire coast, and with it the regional economy – which has made tourism all the more important. One of the most appealing destinations is the Txai Resort, set amid a 100-hectare coconut grove which looks like a soft green pillow from the air. In the language of the Kaxinawa Indians, "Txai" means "companion", and in the spirit of this philosophy every guest is received as a family friend. The bungalows, built up on stilts, have all the distinctive atmosphere of private homes, and are furnished in the snug, rustic style of Bahia – no superfluous frills, dark wood, light fabrics, and colour-washed walls. The moment you wake you're looking at a picture-book natural setting, through the gossamer haze of the mosquito net. You can idle the day away on a recliner or at the beach, and succumb to the rhythms of Brazilian music in the evening. The resort supports reafforestation projects and offers natural history excursions into the surrounding area. There's also a spa for relaxing massages, and yoga classes, and a restaurant where you can feed your eyes on the fabulous view as you dine on phenomenal fish.

Book to pack: "Gabriela, Clove and Cinnamon" by Jorge Amado

Txai Resort
Rodovia Ilhéus Itacaré, km 48
Itacaré
Bahia
Brazil
CEP 45530 000
Tel: + 55 (73) 2101 5000
E-mail: central.reservas@txairesorts.com
Website: www.txairesorts.com

DIRECTIONS	15 km/10 miles south of Itacaré, 50 minutes by road from Ilhéus airport (transfer can be arranged on request)
RATES	$$$$
ROOMS	38 suites
FOOD	Restaurant serving Bahian dishes such as "moqueca" (seafood and fish)
HISTORY	The hotel is located on an ancient coconut and cocoa farm
X-FACTOR	It's like spending your vacation with good friends

Im Garten Eden

Itacaré liegt im Süden von Bahia, direkt an der Kakaoküste – und wurde dank des »schwarzen Goldes« Mitte des 19. Jahrhunderts berühmt und zum größten Exporthafen der Region. Dem Kakao-Boom setzte sogar Brasiliens großer Dichter Jorge Amado mit seinem Roman »Gabriela wie Zimt und Nelken« ein Denkmal – Amado stammt selbst aus der Gegend, er wurde auf einer Kakaoplantage in der Nähe von Ilhéus geboren. Seit 1989 jedoch zerstört ein Pilz Jahr für Jahr fast die gesamte Ernte entlang der Küste und drückt die Wirtschaft zu Boden – umso wichtiger wird der Tourismus. Eine der sympathischsten Adressen ist das Txai Resort inmitten eines 100 Hektar großen Kokoshains, der aus der Vogelperspektive wie ein weiches, grünes Kissen aussieht. In der Sprache der Kaxinawa-Indianer bedeutet »Txai« so viel wie »Gefährte«, und dieser Philosophie zufolge wird hier jeder Gast wie ein Freund der Familie empfangen. Die auf Stelzen gebauten Bungalows besitzen das Flair eines Privathauses, sind im rustikal-gemütlichen Stil Bahias eingerichtet – ohne viel Schnickschnack, mit dunklem Holz, hellen Stoffen und bunt getünchten Wänden. Schon beim Aufwachen blickt man in eine Bilderbuchnatur, vor der das Moskitonetz wie ein zarter Nebel hängt, lässt den Tag auf der Sonnenliege oder am Strand verstreichen und sich abends vom Rhythmus brasilianischer Musik einfangen. Zudem unterstützt das Resort Aufforstungsprojekte und bietet naturkundliche Ausflüge in die Umgebung an, besitzt ein Spa für entspannende Massagen und Yogastunden sowie ein Restaurant, in dem man nicht nur fantastischen Fisch, sondern auch einen fantastischen Ausblick genießt.

Buchtipp: »Gabriela wie Zimt und Nelken« von Jorge Amado

Au jardin d'Éden

Itacaré est située au sud de Bahia, sur la Côte du cacao. Celui-ci a fait sa fortune au milieu du XIXe siècle et l'a transformée en plus grand port d'exportation de la région. Le grand écrivain brésilien Jorge Amado, lui-même né dans une plantation à proximité d'Ilhéus, a d'ailleurs dressé un monument au cacao avec son roman « Gabriela, girofle et cannelle ». Cependant, depuis 1989, une maladie dite « balai de la sorcière » détruit les plantations. Sur le plan économique, le tourisme acquiert donc une importance capitale. Le Txai Resort est l'une des adresses les plus sympathiques. Il est situé au milieu d'une cocoteraie de 100 hectares – vue du ciel, elle ressemble à un grand coussin vert. Dans la langue des Indiens Kaxinava, « Txai » signifie « compagnon », et chaque hôte est vraiment reçu comme un ami de la famille. Les bungalows sur pilotis ont l'atmosphère de maisons particulières, ils sont aménagés dans le style bahianais tout de simplicité rustique et de confort, avec des bois sombres, des étoffes claires et des murs aux vives couleurs. Dès que l'on ouvre les yeux le matin, on distingue une végétation enchanteresse derrière le fin voilage de la moustiquaire ; on passe la journée sur une chaise longue ou à la plage et la soirée à écouter, captivé, des rythmes brésiliens. L'hôtel soutient des projets de reboisement et propose des expéditions d'étude aux alentours. Il possède aussi un centre de remise en forme qui offre des massages et des cours de yoga, ainsi qu'un restaurant dans lequel on peut déguster un poisson exquis en jouissant d'une vue fantastique.

Livre à emporter : « Gabriela, girofle et cannelle » de Jorge Amado

ANREISE	15 Kilometer südlich von Itacaré gelegen, 50 Fahrtminuten vom Flughafen Ilhéus entfernt (Transfer auf Wunsch)
PREIS	$$$$
ZIMMER	38 Suiten
KÜCHE	Restaurant mit bahianischen Gerichten wie »moqueca« (Meeresfrüchte & Fisch)
GESCHICHTE	Das Hotel befindet sich auf dem Anwesen einer ehemaligen Kokosnuss- und Kakaofarm
X-FAKTOR	Ferien wie bei guten Freunden

ACCÈS	Situé à 15 kilomètres au sud d'Itacaré, à 50 minutes de l'aéroport Ilhéus (transfert sur demande)
PRIX	$$$$
CHAMBRE	38 suites
RESTAURATION	Le restaurant propose des spécialités bahianaises comme la « moqueca » (fruits de mer et poisson)
HISTOIRE	L'hôtel se trouve sur une ancienne exploitation de noix de coco et de cacao
LES « PLUS »	Passer les vacances chez des amis

A hut beneath palm trees...
Uxua Casa Hotel & Spa, Bahia

Uxua Casa Hotel & Spa, Bahia

A hut beneath palm trees

Where the green rainforest of Bahia borders the pale blue sea, there lies the little village of Trancoso: a few colourful huts, a whitewashed chapel, and between them a large open space to which all the inhabitants flock in the evening. Since 2009 this place of genuine, original Brazilian joie de vivre has been the site of a highly successful hotel experiment conceived by the fashion designer Wilbert Das. He has restored eleven "casas" in the village taking maximum consideration of the existing materials – beach loungers made from old fishing boats, water pipes carved from tree trunks and lamps woven from flotsam. His creativity in handling simple materials and collaboration with the artisans of the village are strokes of luck for the guests: once here in Uxua Casa, they are authentically immersed in an ancient place, but do not have to get along without luxurious amenities. The food, too, is part of this remix: the Surinam cherry, for example, which grows here everywhere, appears in many dishes. With a view of the aquamarine Atlantic, a path trodden down to the beach and one of the most beautiful village squares in Brazil, this hotel truly provides a best-of selection of genuine experiences. Its name is therefore the most common summary given by guests: in the language of the Pataxó Indians, "uxua" means "wonderful".

Book to pack: "By the River Piedra I Sat Down and Wept" by Paulo Coelho

Uxua Casa Hotel & Spa
Trancoso, Bahia
Brazil
Tel: + 55 (73) 3668 2277
E-mail: info@uxua.com
Website: www.uxua.com

DIRECTIONS	On the Quadrado, the main square of Trancoso, about half-an-hour's drive from Porto Seguro Airport
RATES	$$$
ROOMS	11 casas with one to three bedrooms
FOOD	Fresh, delicious dishes from the regional cuisine of Bahia, with lots of fish and organic vegetables
HISTORY	In 2005 the designer Wilbert Das came to Trancoso for the first time, and in 2009 he realised his vision of a relaxed house beneath palm trees
X-FACTOR	The pool laid with 40,000 pieces of aventurine quartz – a wonderful green stone that is said to have healing powers

Eine Hütte unter Palmen

Wo der grüne Regenwald von Bahia ans hellblaue Meer grenzt, liegt das kleine Dorf Trancoso: ein paar bunte Hütten, eine weiß getünchte Kapelle und dazwischen ein großer, freier Platz, auf dem sich abends die ganze Einwohnerschaft tummelt. An diesem Ort urtümlicher brasilianischer Lebensfreude steht seit 2009 auch ein äußerst geglücktes Hotelexperiment, das sich der Modedesigner Wilbert Das ausgedacht hatte. Er hat elf »casas« des Dorfes mit maximaler Rücksicht auf die vorhandenen Materialien restauriert – Strandliegen aus alten Fischerbooten gebaut, Wasserleitungen aus Baumstämmen geschnitzt und Lampen aus Treibgut geflochten. Seine Kreativität im Umgang mit simplen Werkstoffen und die Zusammenarbeit mit den Handwerkern im Dorf sind ein Glücksfall für den Gast: Einmal im Uxua Casa angekommen, erlebt er hier authentisches Eintauchen in einen uralten Ort, ohne auf luxuriöse Annehmlichkeiten verzichten zu müssen. Auch die Küche spielt bei diesem Remix mit, zum Beispiel taucht die Surinamkirsche, die hier überall wächst, in vielen Gerichten auf. Mit Blick auf den tiefblauen Atlantik, einem Trampelpfad zum Strand und einem der schönsten Dorfplätze Brasiliens bietet dieses Hotel wirklich ein Best-of an authentischen Eindrücken. Der Name des Hauses ist deswegen zugleich auch das häufigste Resümee der Gäste hier: »Uxua« bedeutet in der Sprache der Pataxó-Indianer »wunderbar«.

Buchtipp: »Am Ufer des Rio Piedra saß ich und weinte« von Paulo Coelho

Une cabane sous les palmiers

Aux confins de la verte forêt pluviale du Bahia et de l'océan bleu clair se trouve le petit village de Trancoso : quelques cabanes peintes dans des couleurs éclatantes, une chapelle blanchie à la chaux et, au beau milieu, une grande place dégagée sur laquelle tous les habitants du village affluent le soir. Ce lieu qui respire la joie de vivre authentiquement brésilienne est le théâtre depuis 2009 d'une expérience hôtelière très réussie, conçue par Wilbert Das. Ce styliste a restauré onze casas du village en utilisant dans la mesure du possible des matériaux trouvés sur place : des transats ont été fabriqués à partir d'anciennes barques de pêcheurs, des conduites d'eau ont été creusées dans des troncs d'arbres et des lampes ont été créées en tressant des objets rejetés par la mer sur la plage. Que Wilbert Das en ait confié la réalisation à des artisans du village est une chance inouïe pour le visiteur : une fois arrivé à Uxua Casa, il s'immerge véritablement dans un lieu séculaire sans cependant renoncer aux agréments du luxe. La cuisine y va aussi de son remix : par exemple, elle intègre à de nombreux plats la cerise de Cayenne, qui pousse ici partout. Avec vue sur les eaux bleu profond de l'Atlantique, l'accès à la plage par un sentier de terre battue et une des plus belles places de village du Brésil, cet hôtel propose vraiment la quintessence des impressions authentiques. C'est pourquoi le nom de cet établissement tient aussi lieu d'appréciation de la part de la majorité des hôtes : dans la langue des Indiens pataxos, « uxua » signifie « merveilleux ».

Livre à emporter : « Sur le bord de la rivière Piedra » de Paulo Coelho

ANREISE	Am Quadrado, dem Hauptplatz von Trancoso gelegen, vom Flughafen Porto Seguro etwa eine halbe Stunde Fahrt
PREIS	$$$
ZIMMER	11 Casas mit 1–3 Schlafzimmern
KÜCHE	Frische und köstliche Gerichte der regionalen Küche Bahias; mit viel Fisch und biologisch angebautem Gemüse
GESCHICHTE	2005 war der Designer Wilbert Das erstmals in Trancoso, 2009 konnte er hier seine Vision von einem relaxten Haus unter Palmen eröffnen
X-FAKTOR	Der mit 40.000 Aventurin-Quarzen ausgelegte Pool – dieser herrlich grüne Stein soll heilende Kräfte haben

ACCÈS	Situé sur le Quadrado, la place du village de Trancoso, à environ une demi-heure de route de l'aéroport international Porto Seguro
PRIX	$$$
CHAMBRES	11 casas comprenant 1 à 3 chambres
CUISINE	Des plats frais et délicieux du Bahia, avec beaucoup de viande et de légumes bio
HISTOIRE	Après un premier séjour à Trancoso en 2005, le styliste Wilbert Das a pu ouvrir en 2009 l'hôtel décontracté sous les palmiers dont il rêvait
LES « PLUS »	La piscine habillée de 40 000 aventurines, des pierres censées avoir des propriétés curatives

A hideaway in the greenery...
Hotel da Praça, Bahia

Hotel da Praça, Bahia

A hideaway in the greenery

Some places have a very special aura, and Trancoso in Brazil is one of them. 450 years ago Jesuits established themselves here by the sea, and since those times interesting people have come again and again to this beach, lending Trancoso the title of "hippest fishing village in the world". And indeed it was the hippy scene that gave it a new lease of life 40 years ago and celebrated the lightness of being here. This is exactly what the Hotel de Praça is all about, congenially built in a picturesque setting by the architect couple Beatriz Regis Bittencourt and Ricardo Salém. It has a style of construction typical of the region, including a shingle roof and a tropical garden with trees that are hundreds of years old. To practise capoeira here in the late afternoon or watch a game of genuine Brazilian street football and bring the day to a close by enjoying a biri-biri caipirinha in a hammock – what could be a better way of attaining happiness in the Brazilian style? A further happy element is the attention to detail with which the hotel has been fitted out. The suites in the Hotel da Praça all have unique decor with four-poster beds and hand-painted fabrics. At every turn guests can marvel at the works of local artists. For example, the textile artist Mucki Skowronski enlivens the rooms with her gaily colourful bedspreads, and Cris Conde made exclusive tiles bearing motifs from Trancoso. To stay here is to feel the heartbeat of this wonderful place. And it goes without saying that the heart of Trancoso beats to a samba rhythm ...

Book to pack: "Dona Flor and her Two Husbands" by Jorge Amado

Hotel da Praça
Praça Sao Joao, 01, Trancoso
Bahia
Brazil
Tel: + 55 (73) 3668 2121
E-mail: reservas@hoteldapraca.com.br
Website: www.hoteldapraca.com.br

DIRECTIONS	40 km/25 miles south of Porto Seguro international airport. Transfer by ferry (Porto Seguro-Arraial d'Ajuda) and car or by car only
RATES	$
ROOMS	8 apartments, 3 suites
FOOD	Bahian classics with a Japanese touch are served
HISTORY	The hotel was remodelled in 2006 – in response to the new boom at the holiday resort
X-FACTOR	The beach house for special occasions

Ein Versteck im Grünen

Es gibt Orte, die eine ganz besondere Ausstrahlung haben, und genau so einer ist Trancoso in Brasilien. Schon vor 450 Jahren ließen sich Jesuiten genau hier am Meer nieder, und seitdem zieht es immer wieder interessante Menschen an diesen Strand, was dem kleinen Ort schon den Titel »Hippstes Fischerdorf der Welt« einbrachte. Tatsächlich war es die Hippieszene, die vor vierzig Jahren neue Impulse gab und in Trancoso die Leichtigkeit des Seins zelebrierte. Genau darum geht es auch im Hotel de Praça, das von dem Architekten-Duo Beatriz Regis Bittencourt und Ricardo Salém kongenial in die malerische Kulisse gebaut wurde. Dazu gehören eine für die Region typische Bauweise mit einer Dachkonstruktion aus Schindeln ebenso wie der tropische Garten mit jahrhundertealten Bäumen. Hier am späten Nachmittag Capoeira üben oder im Dorf eine Runde echten brasilianischen Straßenfußball erleben und den Tag am Abend mit einem Biri-Biri-Caipirinha in der Hängematte ausklingen lassen – was braucht es mehr für brasilianische Glücksgefühle? Glücklich macht auch das Augenmerk, mit dem das Haus ausgestattet wurde. Die Suiten im Hotel da Praça verfügen alle über ein einzigartiges Dekor mit Himmelbetten und handbemalten Stoffen, und bei jedem Schritt staunt man über die Werke lokaler Künstler. So hat etwa die Textilkünstlerin Mucki Skowronski mit ihren fröhlichen Tagesdecken lebhafte Akzente gesetzt, und Cris Conde schuf dazu exklusive Fliesen mit Motiven aus Trancoso. Wer hier wohnt, lebt also ganz nah am Puls dieses wunderbaren Ortes. Ein Puls, der übrigens natürlich im Sambarhythmus schlägt ...

Buchtipp: »Dona Flor und ihre zwei Ehemänner« von Jorge Amado

Une cachette dans la verdure

Certains endroits sont enveloppés d'une aura bien particulière. Trancoso, au Brésil, en fait partie. Il y a déjà 450 ans, des jésuites se sont installés dans ces lieux, au bord de la mer, et depuis, des personnalités fréquentent continuellement cette plage, ce qui a déjà valu à cette localité le titre de « village de pêcheurs le plus branché au monde ». Il y a 40 ans, les hippies ont effectivement contribué à l'évolution des mœurs et célébré la légèreté de l'être ici même, à Trancoso. C'est justement dans cet esprit que le duo d'architectes Beatriz Regis Bittencourt et Ricardo Salém ont construit dans ce cadre idyllique l'hôtel da Praça, génialement servi par un mode de construction typique de la région avec un toit de bardeaux ainsi que par un jardin tropical abritant des arbres centenaires. Pratiquer la capoeira ici en fin d'après-midi, assister à une partie de vrai football de rue brésilien et achever la journée en beauté en sirotant une caipirinha au biri-biri – est-il besoin de davantage pour combler l'âme brésilienne ? On est également comblé par le soin apporté à l'aménagement de l'établissement. Chacune des suites a son propre cachet, avec des lits à baldaquin et des tissus peints à la main. A chaque pas, on s'émerveille devant les œuvres d'un artiste du cru, comme les couvre-lit hauts en couleurs de la styliste textile Mucki Skowronski, auxquels font à dessein écho des carrelages exclusifs avec des motifs de Trancoso signés Cris Conde. Qui séjourne ici sent son cœur vibrer à l'unisson de ce lieu magique. Un lieu qui vibre bien sûr au rythme de la samba.

Livre à emporter : « Dona Flor et ses deux maris » de Jorge Amado

ANREISE	40 Kilometer südlich des Internationalen Flughafens Porto Seguro gelegen. Transfer per Fähre (Porto Seguro-Arraial d'Ajuda) und Auto oder nur per Auto
PREIS	$
ZIMMER	8 Apartments, 3 Suiten
KÜCHE	Serviert werden bahianische Klassiker mit japanischem Touch
GESCHICHTE	2006 wurde das Hotel neu gestaltet – als Antwort auf den neuen Boom des Ferienortes
X-FAKTOR	Das Strandhaus für besondere Anlässe

ACCÈS	Situé à 40 kilomètres au sud de l'aéroport international de Porto Seguro. Transfert en ferry (Porto Seguro-Arraial d'Ajuda) et voiture ou seulement en voiture
PRIX	$
CHAMBRES	8 appartements, 3 suites
RESTAURATION	Les classiques de la cuisine du Bahia avec une note japonaise
HISTOIRE	En 2006, l'hôtel a été réaménagé en réponse au nouveau boom touristique que connaît cette destination de vacances
LES « PLUS »	La maison sur la plage pour les grandes occasions

Blue peace and tranquillity...
Estrela d'Água, Bahia

Estrela d'Água, Bahia

Blue peace and tranquillity

Trancoso has always been a place of refuge. The small town was founded in the mid-16th century by Jesuits wanting to afford the indigenous peoples some protection from the colonial conquerors. In the 1970s the hippies and drop-outs discovered it, finding in this tranquil settlement between the ocean and the rainforest the perfect antidote to the bustle of São Paulo. And then there were the artists, seeking inspiration in the light and magic of this coast. Travellers can find happiness here too. Trancoso has miles of perfect beaches, among the finest in all Brazil, and it also has the Estrela d'Água – a Pousada that is virtually paradise. Right on the famous Praia dos Nativos in grounds of 23,000 square metres (247,500 square feet) studded with palms and pink hibiscus, it has suites and bungalows with all the cheery charm of the Bahia. To gaze at the pool and the ocean is to discover whole new unguessed-at shades of blue. You stroll down steps with gleaming red or blue rails, relax on turquoise sofas, and recline on cushions patterned with sun-yellow flowers. But there's no risk of colour overkill, thanks to the quiet tonalities of the understated interiors – dark parquet and dark wood, plain lines and plain materials, lots of room and plenty of space. If anywhere could possibly be better to relax than the hammock, it can only be the spacious veranda, dappled by sunlight through the roof that leaves magical patterns of stripes on the seats and recliners. And if you really do need movement, there are fitness or yoga classes, a tennis court close by, or of course the blue Atlantic to go diving in.

Book to pack: "The Brazilians" by Joseph A. Page

Estrela d'Água
Estrada Arraial d'Ajuda-Trancoso
Trancoso – Porto Seguro
Bahia
Brazil
CEP 45 818 000
Tel: + 55 (73) 3668 1172
E-mail: reservas@estreladagua.com.br
Website: www.estreladagua.com.br

DIRECTIONS	Situated 40 km/25 miles south of Porto Seguro international airport. Transfer by ferry (Porto Seguro-Arrial d'Ajuda) and road or by road only. There is a heliport 10 km/6 miles from the hotel
RATES	$$$
ROOMS	1 duplex bungalow, 7 bungalows, 20 suites
FOOD	The restaurant has a dream veranda and serves mainly regional cuisine
HISTORY	A beach resort in a former drop-out heaven
X-FACTOR	The colours are simply unbelievable!

Our little realm...
Pousada Etnia, Bahia

Pousada Etnia, Bahia

Our little realm

There are times when your ticket quite clearly reads "Porto Seguro, Brazil" – and all the same you land in the oriental world of the Arabian Nights, or on the shores of the Mediterranean. In fact you're on vacation at the Pousada Etnia, a charming retreat tucked away in a dreamy Trancoso park. It entirely lives up to its name, and the bungalows and apartments are conceived in homage to a variety of places and cultures. The "Trancoso" is the bungalow closest in feel to the Brazilian setting. It is simply furnished with rattan armchairs, native wood, and light-hued fabrics, and its understated grace sets off the exuberance of the outside world on the doorstep all the more. Dark furniture reminiscent of colonial times, animal prints, and African-inspired art are the hallmark of the "Tribal" bungalow, with its discreet safari mood. In the "Cottage" you can enjoy the bright and breezy style of tropical islands such as the Seychelles, with just a hint of the English south. If other European moods are what you crave, relax in the "Mediterráneo" on the blue-and-white cushions and marvel at the model sailing ships. Finally, all the magic of the Orient is yours in the "Maroccos" bungalow with its typical pointed doors, the golden gleam of brass, and hand-woven carpets. The proprietors of Etnia aim to transcend borders and create a cosmopolitan kaleidoscope where the best of various cultures is juxtaposed and possesses a new fascination in the encounter. The hotel shop sells antiques and art to match the styles – and throws in a boundless enthusiasm for the Pousada philosophy for free.
Book to pack: "The Devil to Pay in the Backlands" by João Guimarães Rosa

Pousada Etnia

Rua Principal

Trancoso – Porto Seguro

Bahia

Brazil

CEP 458 18 000

Tel: + 55 (73) 3668 1137

Fax: + 55 (73) 3668 1843

E-mail: etniabrasil@etniabrasil.com.br

Website: www.etniabrasil.com.br

DIRECTIONS	Situated 40 km/25 miles south of Porto Seguro international airport. Transfer by ferry (Porto Seguro-Arrial d'Ajuda) and road or by road only
RATES	$
ROOMS	8 bungalows
FOOD	Light cuisine in the poolside restaurant. The bar is famed for its drinks
HISTORY	Opened in December 2002
X-FACTOR	A meeting place for the world's cultures

Unsere kleine Welt

Manchmal steht auf dem Flugschein ganz deutlich »Porto Seguro, Brasilien« – und man landet doch in tausendundeiner Nacht des Orients oder an den Gestaden des Mittelmeers ... Dann nämlich, wenn man seinen Urlaub in der Pousada Etnia verbringt, einer charmanten Anlage mitten in einem verwunschenen Park von Trancoso. Sie macht ihrem Namen alle Ehre und hat die Bungalows und Apartments als Hommage an unterschiedliche Destinationen und Kulturen entworfen. Der brasilianischen Umgebung am nächsten ist der Bungalow »Trancoso«, der schlicht mit Rattansesseln, einheimischem Holz und hellen Stoffen eingerichtet ist und dank seiner Zurückhaltung die üppige Natur vor der Tür nur noch besser zur Geltung bringt. Dunkle und an Kolonialzeiten erinnernde Möbel, Animalprints und afrikanisch inspirierte Kunst zeichnen die Wohnung »Tribal« aus und sorgen für dezentes Safari-Feeling; das luftige Flair tropischer Inseln wie der Seychellen, gemischt mit einem Hauch Südengland, herrscht im »Cottage«. Wer sich nach weiteren europäischen Einflüssen sehnt, zieht in die Unterkunft »Mediterrâneo« und entspannt dort auf blau-weiß gestreiften Kissen oder bewundert Segelschiffmodelle. Die Magie des Orients schließlich besitzt der Bungalow »Maroccos« – mit den typischen, spitz zulaufenden Türen, goldglänzendem Messing und handgewebten Teppichen. Es geht den Besitzern von Etnia darum, Grenzen aufzuheben und ein kosmopolitisches Kaleidoskop zu schaffen, in dem das Beste aus verschiedenen Kulturkreisen unvermittelt aufeinandertrifft und gerade deshalb so faszinierend ist. Im hoteleigenen Shop werden passende Antiquitäten und Kunst verkauft – die Begeisterung für die Philosophie der Pousada gibt es gratis mit dazu.

Buchtipp: »Krieg im Sertao« von João Guimarães Rosa

Notre petit royaume

On peut très bien lire « Porto Seguro, Brésil » sur le billet d'avion et se retrouver dans une ambiance de Mille et Une Nuits ou sur les rivages de la Méditerranée... C'est ce qui arrive si l'on passe ses vacances à la Pousada Etnia, un hôtel charmant situé dans un parc ravissant à Trancoso. Son nom est tout un programme et, de fait, les bungalows et les appartements ont été conçus et décorés en hommage à divers pays et cultures. Le bungalow « Trancoso » se rapproche le plus de l'environnement brésilien avec ses fauteuils de rotin, ses essences locales et ses étoffes claires – sa sobriété met en valeur la végétation exubérante qui s'épanouit au pied de la porte. Le bungalow « Tribal », quant à lui, est doté de meubles sombres évoquant l'ère coloniale, d'impressions animalières et d'œuvres inspirées de l'art africain. Le « Cottage » marie l'atmosphère des îles heureuses et des accents cosy du Sud anglais. Celui qui désire d'autres influences européennes s'installe dans le bungalow « Mediterrâneo », se détend sur des coussins rayés bleu et blanc ou admire des maquettes de voiliers. Et enfin le bungalow « Maroccos » avec ses portes en ogive, ses laitons étincelants et ses tapis tissés à la main offre toute la magie de l'Orient. Les propriétaires d'Etnia veulent abolir les frontières et créer une mosaïque cosmopolite réunissant le meilleur de ce que les diverses cultures ont à offrir, et cette rencontre est fascinante. La boutique de l'hôtel vend les antiquités et les œuvres d'art correspondantes – l'enthousiasme pour la philosophie qui règne en ces lieux est gracieusement offert en sus.

Livre à emporter : « Diadorim » de João Guimarães Rosa

ANREISE	40 Kilometer südlich des Internationalen Flughafens Porto Seguro gelegen. Transfer per Fähre (Porto Seguro-Arrial d'Ajuda) und Auto oder nur per Auto
PREIS	$
ZIMMER	8 Bungalows
KÜCHE	Leichte Küche am Pool-Restaurant. Die Bar ist für ihre Drinks berühmt
GESCHICHTE	Im Dezember 2002 eröffnet
X-FAKTOR	Ein Treffpunkt der Kulturen

ACCÈS	Situé à 40 kilomètres au sud de l'aéroport international de Porto Seguro. Transfert en ferry (Porto Seguro-Arrial d'Ajuda) et voiture ou seulement en voiture
PRIX	$
CHAMBRES	8 bungalows
RESTAURATION	Cuisine légère au restaurant de la piscine. Le bar est renommé pour ses cocktails
HISTOIRE	Ouvert depuis décembre 2002
LES « PLUS »	Le rendez-vous des cultures

A hidden paradise...
Vila Naiá – Paralelo 17°, Bahia

Vila Naiá – Paralelo 17°, Bahia

A hidden paradise

This paradise isn't one with an address. There's no zip code, no streeet name, no house number. No guidebook or map will help you find it – to get to Vila Naiá, you need the sixth sense for orientation that a pilot, rally driver, or helmsman has. It's a small resort, opened in September 2004, on the Atlantic coast near Corumbau, on the edge of the Monte Pascoal National Park and a fishing reservation where only the indigenous population are allowed out to sea. Bahia, otherwise so temperamental, seems worlds away. All you can hear is the breeze in the palm fronds and the wavelets lapping on the beach. The air you breathe has a mild salty tang, and the sun is warm on your skin. For ten years, architect Renato Marques and owner Renata Mellão worked at the Vila Naiá concept, till the buildings were as plain and true to the local spirit as the natural world all around – not too much the ecological resort, and not too understated on the luxuries for guests who like their creature comforts. The four suites and four houses are simple of line, panelled in dark wood within, and not over-furnished. The only strong colours added to the natural hues are the chairs, hammocks and throws. The kitchen is a no-frills affair as well. At Vila Naiá, Maria Alice Solimene prepares typical Brazilian specialities and plans her menu to fit the fishermen's catch that morning and according to what the garden provides. Those with even more purist tastes can eat at Rafael Rosa, where the manager and second maitre is probably the only chef in the country to be serving "raw living food".

Book to pack: "Captains of the Sands" by Jorge Amado

Vila Naiá – Paralelo 17°

Corumbau

Bahia

Brazil

Tel: + 55 (11) 3063 2023

E-mail: reservas@vilanaia.com.br

Website: www.vilanaia.com.br

DIRECTIONS	Situated 230 km/140 miles south of Porto Seguro airport. Transfer by light aircraft (20 minutes, US$ 323), Landrover (approx. 4 hours, US$ 145) or Landrover and boat (2 hours 45 minutes, US$ 340)
RATES	$$$–$$$$
ROOMS	4 suites, 3 houses and 1 double house
FOOD	Brazilian cuisine and "raw living food"
HISTORY	Ten years in the making, it opened in 2004
X-FACTOR	Right in the heart of nature

Das versteckte Paradies

Das Paradies hat keine genaue Adresse – keine Straße, keine Hausnummer, keine Postleitzahl. Bei seiner Entdeckung nützt kein Reiseführer und keine Landkarte – wer zur Vila Naiá möchte, muss dem Orientierungssinn des Piloten, Fahrers oder Bootsmannes vertrauen. Das kleine im September 2004 eröffnete Resort liegt an der Atlantikküste bei Corumbau; am Rand des Nationalparks Monte Pascoal und eines Fischreservats, in dem nur die Einheimischen hinaus aufs Meer fahren dürfen. Hier scheint das sonst so temperamentvolle Bahia Welten entfernt zu sein; man hört den Wind in den Palmen und die Wellen an den Strand rauschen, atmet salzig-sanfte Luft und spürt die Sonne auf der Haut. Zehn Jahre lang haben Architekt Renato Marques und Besitzerin Renata Mellão am Konzept der Vila Naiá getüftelt, bis die Häuser genau so schlicht und ursprünglich wie die umliegende Natur waren, nicht zu sehr in Richtung »Öko-Resort« abdrifteten und nicht zu wenig Luxus für anspruchsvolle Gäste bieten. Die vier Suiten und vier Häuser wurden innen mit dunklem Holz verkleidet und zeigen einfache Linien und sparsame Möblierung – einige bunte Stühle, Hängematten und Decken sind die einzigen Akzente inmitten der Naturtöne. Ohne Schnörkel kommt auch die Küche aus: In der Vila Naiá kocht Maria Alice Solimene typisch brasilianische Spezialitäten und richtet ihre Menükarte danach aus, was die Fischer jeden Morgen anliefern oder der hauseigene Biogarten hergibt. Wer es noch puristischer mag, sollte bei Rafael Rosa essen: Der Manager der Anlage und zugleich ihr zweiter Maître serviert als wahrscheinlich einziger Küchenchef des Landes »raw living food«, ausschließlich rohe und naturbelassene Gerichte.

Buchtipp: »Herren des Strandes« von Jorge Amado

Un paradis caché

Le paradis n'a pas d'adresse – pas de rue, pas de numéro, pas de code postal. Pour le découvrir, les guides et les cartes ne servent à rien. Celui qui veut se rendre à la Vila Naiá doit se fier au sens de l'orientation du pilote d'avion, du chauffeur de voiture ou du capitaine de bateau. Le petit hôtel, ouvert seulement depuis septembre 2004, se trouve sur la côte atlantique près de Corumbau, en bordure du parc national de Monte Pascoal et d'une réserve maritime où seuls les autochtones ont le droit de pénétrer. La ville trépidante de Bahia semble à des années-lumière. Ici on entend le murmure du vent dans les palmiers et le grondement des vagues sur la plage, on respire l'air marin et l'on sent la caresse du soleil sur sa peau. Pendant dix ans, l'architecte Renato Marques et la propriétaire Renata Mellão ont travaillé sur le concept de la Vila Naiá, jusqu'à ce que les maisons soient aussi simples et authentiques que la nature environnante, sans tomber dans l'écologie à outrance mais en offrant assez de luxe pour les clients exigeants. Les quatre suites et les quatre maisons habillés de bois sombre ont des lignes sobres et sont décorés sans exubérance – les chaises, hamacs et couvertures sont les seuls accents de couleur parmi les tons naturels. La cuisine est elle aussi dénuée de fioritures : à la Vila Naiá, Maria Alice Solimene prépare des spécialités typiquement brésiliennes en fonction des poissons que lui apportent les pêcheurs tous les matins ou en fonction des produits du jardin bio. Si vous êtes encore plus puriste, ne manquez pas d'aller manger chez Rafael Rosa : le gérant de l'hôtel, qui est en même temps le deuxième maître queux, est probablement le seul chef du pays à servir une « raw living food », des plats exclusivement crus et naturels.

Livre à emporter : « Capitaines des sables » de Jorge Amado

ANREISE	230 Kilometer südlich des Flughafens Porto Seguro gelegen. Transfer per Kleinflugzeug (20 Minuten, US$ 323), Landrover (4 Stunden, US$ 145) oder Landrover und Boot (2 Stunden 45 Minuten, US$ 340)
PREIS	$$$–$$$$
ZIMMER	4 Suiten, 3 Häuser und 1 Doppelhaus
KÜCHE	Brasilianische Gerichte und »raw living food«
GESCHICHTE	Nach zehnjähriger Entwicklung 2004 eröffnet
X-FAKTOR	Im Herzen der Natur

ACCÈS	Situé à 230 kilomètres au sud de l'aéroport de Porto Seguro. Transfert en petit avion (20 minutes, US$ 323), en Landrover (env. 4 heures, US$ 145) ou en Landrover et en bateau (2 heures 45 minutes, US$ 340)
PRIX	$$$–$$$$
CHAMBRES	4 suites, 3 maisons et 1 maison double
RESTAURATION	Plats brésiliens et « raw living food »
HISTOIRE	Ouvert depuis 2004 après une conception de dix ans
LES « PLUS »	On ne saurait être encore plus proche de la nature

A retreat for beachcombers
Fazenda São Francisco do Corumbau, Bahia

Fazenda São Francisco
do Corumbau, Bahia

A retreat for beachcombers

Bahia may be one of the liveliest, most temperamental of Brazil's federal states, but it also honours the principle of the laid-back, leisurely pace. Whether at the office, in the supermarket, or on the street, no one gets hot under the collar if they can help it, and the local saying even has it that anyone running in Bahia must be either a thief or someone who's lost something important beyond belief. The lightness of being is especially infectious if you visit the south of the region, where the country is flat as a pancake and the white beaches and palm groves reach right to the horizon. You'll forget the very concept of "stress" the moment you dig your toes into the sand, pick up your first coconut, or simply feel the salt water tingle on your skin. To be a guest at the Fazenda São Francisco do Corumbau is to slip into a time capsule – your alarm clock, watch, and mobile phone may as well stay in the suitcase. The estate, located between Porto Seguro and Prado, was formerly a coconut plantation; but for roughly the last 30 years the 5,000 or so palms have simply been a dream backdrop, and a perfect contrast to the white sand. The six suites are a rich composition in colour, with exotic blooms on the sofa cushions, red drapes hung before lime-green walls, shower curtains in every tropical colour of your dreams, and bold tartan bedspreads to make even a Scotsman envious. The Fazenda has a fish restaurant and a first-rate programme of sporting options, making it truly a place to chill and enjoy – a feel-good retreat to savour to the full.

Book to pack: "Macunaíma" by Mario de Andrade

Fazenda São Francisco do Corumbau Ponta do Corumbau Bahia Brazil Tel: + 55 (11) 3078 4411 Fax: + 55 (73) 3294 2250 E-mail: corumbau@corumbau.com.br Website: www.corumbau.com.br	DIRECTIONS — Situated between Porto Seguro and Prado, 1,000 km/ 625 miles north of Rio de Janeiro. The transfer from Porto Seguro is organised (Landrover for 4 people: US$ 365 or helicopter for 3 people: US$ 1,435) RATES — $$$ ROOMS — 6 suites (2 in the main building, 4 in bungalows) FOOD — Fresh fish and Brazilian specialities HISTORY — In the 80s, a coconut plantation was made over into a small hotel X-FACTOR — A vacation as peaceful as it gets

Für Strandläufer

Bahia gehört zu den temperamentvollsten Bundesstaaten Brasiliens, doch zugleich macht man hier die Gelassenheit und Langsamkeit zum Lebensprinzip. Egal, ob im Büro, im Supermarkt oder auf der Straße – niemand lässt sich so leicht aus der Ruhe bringen, und die Einheimischen behaupten sogar, wer in Bahia renne, sei entweder ein Dieb oder müsse gerade etwas unglaublich Wichtiges verloren haben. Von der Leichtigkeit des Seins lassen sich Besucher vor allem im Süden der Region anstecken; dort, wo das Land wie flachgebügelt daliegt und sich weiße Strände und Palmenhaine bis hinter den Horizont ziehen. Begriffe wie »Stress« oder »Hektik« tilgt man in dem Moment aus seinem Wortschatz, in dem man zum ersten Mal die Füße im Sand vergräbt, die erste Kokosnuss vom Boden aufhebt oder den ersten Spritzer Salzwasser auf der Haut spürt. Die Fazenda São Francisco do Corumbau schenkt ihren Gästen Ferien wie in einem Zeitloch – Wecker, Armbanduhren oder Handys bleiben wie von selbst im Koffer. Ursprünglich war das Anwesen zwischen Porto Seguro und Prado eine Kokosplantage; seit rund 30 Jahren sind die 5.000 Palmen aber nur noch Traumkulisse und perfekter Kontrast zum weißen Strand. Für ordentlich Farbe wird in den sechs Suiten gesorgt – in den Räumen wachsen exotische Blumen auf den Sofakissen, vor lindgrünen Wänden wehen rote Gardinen, die Duschvorhänge sind so bunt wie ein Südseetraum, und auf die groß karierten Bettdecken wären sogar Schotten neidisch. Die Fazenda ist auch dank ihres Fischrestaurants und ihres Sportprogramms ein echtes Gute-Laune-Ziel – und eines, das man in aller Seelenruhe genießen kann.

Buchtipp: »Macunaíma« von Mario de Andrade

Eau, sable et cocotiers

Les Bahianais sont bien connus pour leur tempérament fougueux, pourtant la tranquillité et la lenteur ont été élevées ici en principes de vie. Au bureau, au supermarché ou dans la rue, les gens perdent rarement leur sang-froid, et les autochtones prétendent même que celui qui court à Bahia a volé quelque chose ou perdu un objet auquel il tenait énormément. Cette légèreté de l'être est contagieuse, surtout au sud de la région, là où le pays semble plat et lisse, là où les plages de sable blanc et les bosquets de cocotiers s'étirent jusqu'à l'horizon. Dès le moment où l'on plonge avec délice ses pieds dans le sable fin, où l'on ramasse la première noix de coco et où l'eau salée touche la peau, des mots comme « stress » et « nervosité » disparaissent du vocabulaire. À la Fazenda São Francisco do Corumbau, le temps n'existe plus – les réveils, les montres et les portables restent dans les valises. À l'origine la propriété située entre Porto Seguro et Prado était une plantation de coprah : depuis une trentaine d'années, une maison s'y élève et les 5 000 palmiers qui plantent un décor de rêve se marient avec bonheur au sable blanc. Ici la couleur est reine : à l'intérieur des suites, des fleurs exotiques s'épanouissent sur les coussins des canapés, des rideaux rouges se déploient sur des murs vert tilleul, les rideaux de douche sont aussi colorés qu'un rêve des mers du Sud et les Écossais apprécieraient sans aucun doute les jetés de lit à grands carreaux. Avec son restaurant aux spécialités de poisson et son programme sportif, la Fazenda est aussi un lieu où règne la bonne humeur – et on peut s'y détendre en toute quiétude.

Livre à emporter : « Macunaíma » de Mario de Andrade

ANREISE	Zwischen Porto Seguro und Prado gelegen, 1.000 Kilometer nördlich von Rio de Janeiro. Transfer ab Porto Seguro wird organisiert (Landrover für 4 Personen: US$ 365 oder Helikopter für 3 Personen: US$ 1.435)
PREIS	$$$
ZIMMER	6 Suiten (2 im Haupthaus, 4 in Bungalows)
KÜCHE	Frischer Fisch und brasilianische Spezialitäten
GESCHICHTE	Aus einer Kokosplantage wurde in den 1980er-Jahren ein kleines Hotel
X-FAKTOR	Ferien in aller Ruhe

ACCÈS	Situé entre Porto Seguro et Prado, à 1000 kilomètres au nord de Rio de Janeiro. Le transfert est organisé à partir de Porto Seguro (Landrover pour 4 personnes : US$ 365 ou hélicoptère pour 3 personnes : US$ 1435)
PRIX	$$$
CHAMBRES	6 suites (2 dans la maison principale, 4 dans des bungalows)
RESTAURATION	Poisson frais et spécialités brésiliennes
HISTOIRE	Une plantation de cocotiers transformée en hôtel au cours des années 1980
LES « PLUS »	Des vacances que rien ne peut troubler

The quiet heart of Rio...
Hotel Santa Teresa, Rio de Janeiro

Hotel Santa Teresa, Rio de Janeiro

The quiet heart of Rio

No need to worry: the Santa Teresa quarter above the city centre is safe and quiet. Once the haunt of artists and hippies, today it is the cultural and historic heart of Rio de Janeiro. Among all this lies one of the best hotels in South America, where guests can sense the glorious days of the cocoa and coffee trade. What was once the mansion of a coffee plantation has been converted into intimate five-star accommodation in urban ethno-style from top to bottom. Everything here breathes the spirit of the original district: no hurry! A perfect address for visitors who want to discover a new Rio, far from the ostentatious bustle of the beach. Here in Santa Teresa, between mango and apricot trees, time has stood still and neo-colonial charm lives on. This is exactly the right ambience to parade a white linen suit in the tropical garden and sip a red-berry caipirinha while watching the mico monkeys that are among the hotel's regular guests. And the panoramic view of the famous bay of Rio! Many of the beauties who spend the day down there come up to the hotel in the evening, as its bar has become one of the city's high-class hotspots. Of course there is still cocoa here – but mainly in the spa, which offers treatments with cocoa butter and Brazil-nut butter, an experience to give you a melting feeling and the energy for excursions in the vibrant metropolis below.

Book to pack: "Brazil" by John Updike

Hotel Santa Teresa Rua Almirante Alexandrino 660 Santa Teresa 20241-260 Rio de Janeiro, RJ Brazil Tel: + 55 (21) 3380 0200 E-mail: reservas@santateresahotel.com Website: www.santa-teresa-hotel.com	**DIRECTIONS** 18 km/11 miles from Galeão/Antônio Carlos Jobim International Airport
	RATES $$$
	ROOMS 27 rooms, 13 suites, 1 loft
	FOOD The outstanding Restaurant Térèze combines French cuisine with the aromas of Brazil
	HISTORY Santa Teresa, once a coffee baron's villa, opened as a hotel in 2009. What is now the bar was once the workers' quarters
	X-FACTOR After a break of a few years, it's running again: the legendary Bonde, the venerable yellow tram, passes close to the hotel and is the finest way of arriving

Das ruhige Herz von Rio

Keine Sorge, das Viertel Santa Teresa oberhalb der City ist
sicher und ruhig. Einst von Künstlern und Hippies bevölkert,
schlägt hier bis heute das kulturelle und historische Herz
von Rio de Janeiro. Mittendrin wartet eines der besten Hotels
Südamerikas, in dem man die glorreiche Zeit des Kakao- und
Kaffeehandels nachfühlen kann. Aus dem einstigen Herren-
haus einer Kaffeeplantage wurde ein intimes Fünf-Sterne-
Haus, das sich ganz einem urbanen Ethnostil verpflichtet
hat. Alles hier verkörpert den Geist des ursprünglichen
Viertels: Keine Eile! Eine perfekte Adresse für Besucher, die
ein neues Rio entdecken möchten, fernab vom protzigen
Treiben am Strand. Hier im Santa Teresa, zwischen Mango-
und Aprikosenbäumen ist die Zeit stehen und ein neokolo-
nialistischer Charme erhalten geblieben. Genau das richtige
Umfeld, um den weißen Leinenanzug im tropischen Garten
auszuführen und bei einem Red-Berry-Caipirinha die Seiden-
äffchen zu beobachten, die zu den Stammgästen des Hotel-
gartens gehören. Oder den Panoramablick auf die berühmte
Bucht von Rio! Viele der Schönheiten, die sich dort tummeln,
werden abends hier heraufkommen, denn die Bar des Hotels
ist ein gediegener Hotspot der Stadt geworden. Kakao gibt es
hier heute natürlich auch noch, allerdings vor allem im Spa,
wo Anwendungen mit Kakao- und Paranussbutter angeboten
werden – ein Erlebnis zum Dahinschmelzen, das Kraft spen-
det für Ausflüge in die pulsierende Metropole unterhalb.
Buchtipp: »Brasilien« von John Updike

Le cœur paisible de Rio

Il n'y a aucune crainte à avoir : Santa Teresa, sur les hau-
teurs de Rio de Janeiro, est un quartier sûr et calme. Ce
cœur culturel et historique de la métropole, abrite l'un des
meilleurs hôtels d'Amérique du Sud, encore empreint de la
grande époque du négoce du café et du cacao. L'ancienne
maison de maître d'une plantation de café a été transformée
en hôtel 5 étoiles de charme, entièrement aménagé dans le
style ethno-urbain. L'esprit des artistes et hippies qui peu-
plaient autrefois le quartier plane encore sur les lieux, où
l'on fait l'éloge de la lenteur ! C'est l'adresse idéale pour tous
ceux qui veulent découvrir un autre Rio, loin de la frime des
plages. Au Santa Teresa, parmi les manguiers et les abrico-
tiers, le temps s'est arrêté : dans ce cadre qui a conservé son
charme néocolonial, on se plaît à arborer un costume de lin
blanc et à siroter une caipirinha aux fruits rouges tout en
observant les ouistitis qui ont établi domicile dans le jardin
tropical de l'hôtel ou en embrassant du regard la célèbre baie
de Rio ! Nombre des beautés qui s'y bousculent en journée
viendront le soir au Santa Teresa, dont le bar est devenu une
institution qu'il est de bon ton de fréquenter. Si le cacao est
resté d'actualité, il est principalement employé dans le spa,
qui propose des soins à base de ce produit et de beurre de
noix du Brésil – cette expérience à vous faire fondre de
plaisir vous permettra de faire le plein d'énergie avant de
descendre à la découverte de la trépidante métropole qui
s'étale à vos pieds.

Livre à emporter : « Brésil » de John Updike

ANREISE	18 Kilometer vom Galeão/Antônio Carlos Jobim International Airport entfernt
PREIS	$$$
ZIMMER	27 Zimmer, 13 Suiten, 1 Loft
KÜCHE	Das ausgezeichnete Restaurant Térèze verbindet feine französische Küche und brasilianische Aromen
GESCHICHTE	Santa Teresa, einstmals Villa eines Kaffeebarons, wurde im Jahr 2009 als Hotel eröffnet. Die heutige Bar war früher die Unterkunft der Arbeiter
X-FAKTOR	Nach einigen Jahren Pause fährt sie wieder: Die legen-däre Bonde, die würdevolle gelbe Trambahn, kommt nah am Hotel vorbei und ist die schönste Art, hier anzureisen

ACCÈS	L'aéroport international Galeão/Antônio Carlos Jobim est à 18 kilomètres
PRIX	$$$
CHAMBRES	27 chambres, 13 suites, 1 loft
RESTAURATION	L'excellent restaurant Térèze marie le raffinement de la cuisine française et les arômes du Brésil
HISTOIRE	Ancienne maison de maître transformée en hôtel, Santa Teresa a ouvert ses portes en 2009. Le bar a été créé dans les anciens logements des ouvriers
LES « PLUS »	Après plusieurs années d'interruption, le légendaire tramway jaune a repris du service : l'arrivée à l'hôtel par cet élégant tramway laisse un souvenir inoubliable

The Mad Men feeling...

Hotel Fasano Boa Vista, Porto Feliz

Hotel Fasano Boa Vista, Porto Feliz

The Mad Men feeling

To design a hotel in his home town São Paulo was a very special challenge for star architect Isay Weinfeld. The result of his thoughts is a must-see for lovers of architecture – and not only for them. Fasano Boa Vista, situated a little way outside the city, is a remarkable combination of innovative architecture and a traditional experience of nature. Mad Men meets ecological luxury! The restrained façade and classy interior design that looks back to the 1950s and 1960s is undoubtedly a perfect match for all that lies outside the walls. Guests can walk in an untouched landscape, a natural park covering 40 hectares/100 acres with rocks, rainforest, lakes and gardens. For all that, they do not have to do without the amenities of a first-class country resort, which includes two golf courses as well as facilities for horse riding and tennis. Even more impressive, however, is the great tranquillity that is radiated by Weinfeld's design and that makes a stay here almost tantamount to a Zen exercise. To match this, the house philosophy emphasises the simple pleasures in life. The kitchens not only take produce from the hotel's own farm for the supra-regional cuisine – the guests themselves join in, if they so desire. They can borrow garden implements at reception and get to work on the vegetables and fruit grown on the ranch. Follow this up with a refreshing dip in the crystal-clear lake that borders the hotel premises, and what more could anyone want to feel deeply at one with South American joy of life?

Book to pack: "Heliopolis" by James Scudamore

Hotel Fasano Boa Vista
Rodovia Presidente Castello Branco
Km 102.5
Porto Feliz, SP 18540-000
Brazil
Tel: + 55 (15) 3261 9900
E-mail: fbv@fasano.com.br
Website: www.fasano.com.br

DIRECTIONS	Some 103 km/64 miles from São Paulo-Congonhas Airport and 124 km/77 miles from São Paulo-Guarulhos
RATES	$$$
ROOMS	39 rooms and suites. All rooms have a panoramic outlook or a view of the lake or garden
FOOD	Brazilian cooking meets Italian grandezza
HISTORY	At the start of the millennium, the businessman Rogerio Fasano met his favourite architect to talk about realising his big dream. The result, in 2003, was the Hotel Fasano
X-FACTOR	The architecture: to stay in a Weinfeld is like borrowing a Van Gogh

Das Mad-Men-Gefühl

In seiner Heimat São Paulo ein Hotel zu entwerfen, war
für den Stararchitekten Isay Weinfeld eine ganz besondere
Herausforderung. Das Ergebnis seiner Überlegungen ist
heute für Architekturliebhaber unbedingt einen Besuch
wert – und nicht nur für die. Denn das Fasano Boa Vista,
etwas außerhalb der Stadt gelegen, schafft eine ganz besondere Verbindung von innovativer Architektur und tra-
ditionellem Naturerlebnis. Mad Men trifft Ökoluxus! Die
nüchterne Fassade und ein feines Interiordesign, das die
1950er- und 1960er-Jahre zitiert, passen jedenfalls perfekt
zu dem, was vor der Tür wartet. Dort kann sich der Gast in
über 40 Hektar naturbelassenem Park mit Felsen, Urwald,
Seen und Gärten eine ganz ursprüngliche Landschaft erwan-
dern. Dabei muss er trotzdem nicht auf die Annehmlichkeiten eines erstklassigen Country-Resorts verzichten, zu denen
auch zwei Golfplätze, sowie Reit- und Tennisanlagen gehören. Noch viel beeindruckender aber ist die große Ruhe, die
Weinfelds Entwurf ausstrahlt und die einen Aufenthalt hier
beinahe zu einer Zen-Übung macht. Passend dazu hat sich
die Hotelphilosophie den einfachen Freuden des Lebens ver-
schrieben. So bedient man sich hier zum Beispiel nicht nur
der Erzeugnisse der eigenen Farm, um eine superregionale
Küche anbieten zu können – die Gäste dürfen auch gleich
selbst mit Hand anlegen, wenn sie wollen. An der Rezeption
kann man sich Gartengeräte ausleihen und damit dem Ge-
müse und den Früchten der Ranch zu Leibe rücken. Danach
ein erfrischendes Bad im glasklaren See, der an die Anlage
grenzt – was braucht man mehr, um sich der südamerikanischen Lebensfreude tief verbunden zu fühlen?
Buchtipp: »Heliopolis« von James Scudamore

Mad Men Feeling

Concevoir un hôtel dans sa ville natale, São Paulo, était pour
la star de l'architecture Isay Weinfeld un défi singulier. Le
fruit de ses réflexions vaut absolument le détour, et ce pas
uniquement pour les amateurs d'architecture. En effet, le
Fasano Boa Vista, situé en dehors de la ville, jette un pont
de manière originale entre architecture novatrice et classique évasion dans la nature. Mad Men transposé dans le
luxe écologique ! La façade sobre et l'aménagement intérieur
raffiné inspiré des années 1950 et 1960 sont en harmonie
avec le cadre naturel. Dans un parc de plus de 40 hectares,
les hôtes partent à la découverte d'un paysage intact, qui
mêle rochers, forêt pluviale, lacs et jardins. Pas question pour
autant de renoncer aux commodités d'un complexe hôtelier
grand luxe, qui comprend également deux parcours de golf,
un centre équestre et des installations de tennis. On est
cependant davantage impressionné par la sérénité qui émane
de la réalisation de Weinfeld et qui ferait d'un séjour dans
ses murs presque un stage zen. Dans cet esprit, l'hôtel a pour
philosophie les plaisirs simples de la vie, comme la possibilité pour les hôtes de travailler dans le potager et le verger qui
livrent les produits travaillés dans la cuisine suprarégionale :
ils peuvent emprunter à la réception les outils de jardinage
nécessaires pour livrer un corps-à-corps aux fruits et aux
légumes du domaine avant d'enchaîner sur une baignade
rafraîchissante dans les eaux cristallines du lac qui jouxte
l'hôtel. Que faut-il de plus pour se sentir en communion
profonde avec la joie de vivre sud-américaine ?
Livre à emporter : « Fils d'Heliópolis » de James Scudamore

ANREISE	Vom Flughafen São Paulo-Congonhas 103 Kilometer, vom Flughafen São Paulo-Guarulhos 124 Kilometer entfernt
PREIS	$$$
ZIMMER	39 Zimmer und Suiten. Alle Zimmer haben einen Panorama-, See- oder Gartenblick.
KÜCHE	Brasilianische Küche trifft auf italienische Grandezza
GESCHICHTE	Der Unternehmer Rogerio Fasano kam zu Beginn des Jahrtausends zu seinem Lieblingsarchitekten, um mit ihm über seinen großen Traum zu sprechen. Im Jahr 2003 wurde daraus das Hotel Fasano
X-FAKTOR	Die Architektur: In einem Weinfeld gewohnt zu haben, ist wie einen Van Gogh auszuleihen

ACCÈS	L'aéroport de São Paulo-Congonhas est à environ 103 kilomètres, et celui de São Paulo-Guarulhos à 124 kilomètres
PRIX	$$$
CHAMBRES	39 chambres et suites. Toutes ont une vue panora-mique ou donnent sur le lac ou le jardin
RESTAURATION	Cuisine brésilienne mâtinée d'élégance italienne
HISTOIRE	Le chef d'entreprise Rogerio Fasano a fait part de son grand rêve à son architecte préféré. En 2003, Hotel Fasano devenait l'incarnation de ce rêve
LES « PLUS »	L'architecture : séjourner dans un bâtiment signé Weinfeld, c'est comme emprunter un Van Gogh

GARZON

Dinner in the back of beyond.
El Garzón, Garzón

El Garzón, Garzón

Dinner in the back of beyond

In Uruguay a great deal of social life actually takes place on the beach. Those who want to explore the hinterland find themselves amidst untouched nature and profound solitude in many places. In this wilderness, with an archaic, deserted town as a backdrop, the Argentinian star chef Francis Mallmann converted an old shop building into a country house in 2004. Here, far away from disturbances by tourism, the eccentric cook found the right atmosphere for his culinary experiments, which involve much use of an open fire and a massive special barbecue. Little by little this abandoned place became a destination for adventurous gourmets and others who wished to spend a few magical days away from everything. And there are many such people, as everyone who has tried Mallmann's excellent cooking wants to repeat the experience. Today a handful of hotel rooms are available for the purpose, personally furnished in rustic style with a touch of bohemian chic by the visionary himself. Before arriving, guests receive a charming warning from their host: no shopping! No nothing! The ghost town Garzón is still just that, a ghost town, and apart from its natural surroundings the only diversions are a pool and a pretty library. Breakfast is taken in the shady courtyard of the hacienda at the heart of gaucho country, with an acoustic background by cows and hens – could anything be more relaxing? After all, here the excitement happens on the plate.

Book to pack: "A Brief Life" by Juan Carlos Onetti

El Garzón

El Garzón Hotel & Restaurant
By Francis Mallmann & Bodega Garzón
Costa José Ignacio
Garzón
Uruguay
Tel: + 598 (4410) 2811/2809
E-mail: info@restaurantegarzon.com
Website: www.restaurantegarzon.com

DIRECTIONS	In the hinterland north-east of Punta del Este, 40 km/25 miles from José Ignacio. The nearest airport, Aeropuerto de Punta del Este, is 74 km/46miles away
RATES	$$$$
ROOMS	5 rooms, all with stylish black bathrooms
FOOD	Mallmann cooks over a wood fire according to the old Andean "infiernillo" (little hell) method. The meals come to the table on hot iron grids
HISTORY	During a real-estate crisis Mallmann simply bought half of the village of Garzón and made it the centre of his culinary cosmos in 2004
X-FACTOR	A pool beneath palm trees, in the middle of nowhere

Ein Dinner im Nirgendwo

In Uruguay spielen sich weite Teile des gesellschaftlichen Lebens eigentlich am Strand ab. Wer das Hinterland erkunden möchte, sieht sich an vielen Stellen bald von urtümlicher Natur und tiefer Einsamkeit umgeben. Genau in dieser Wildnis, in der archaischen Kulisse einer verlassenen Stadt, hat der argentinische Starkoch Francis Mallmann 2004 ein altes Ladengebäude in ein Landhaus verwandelt. Hier, fernab von allen touristischen Störungen, fand der exzentrische Koch die richtige Atmosphäre für seine kulinarischen Experimente, zu denen viel offenes Feuer und auch ein massiver Spezialgrill gehören. Nach und nach wurde der verlassene Ort so zur Pilgerstätte für wagemutige Gourmets und alle, die ein paar magische Tage im Nirgendwo verbringen wollen. Und das sind viele, denn wer Mallmanns exzellente Küche einmal gekostet hat, möchte dieses Erlebnis gerne wiederholen. Dafür steht heute eine Handvoll Hotelzimmer bereit, die der Visionär persönlich rustikal und mit einem Hauch Boheme-Chic eingerichtet hat. Vor der Anreise erhält man übrigens eine charmante Warnung des Gastgebers: No Shopping! No Nothing! Die Geisterstadt Garzón ist nämlich immer noch eine, und neben der Natur gibt es hier zur Zerstreuung nur einen Pool und eine hübsche Bibliothek. Das Frühstück nimmt man im schattigen Innenhof der Hazienda ein und sitzt da mitten im Herz des Gaucho-Landes, in einer Geräuschkulisse von Kühen und Hähnen – mehr Entspannung geht nicht. Die Aufregung findet hier eben auf den Tellern statt.
Buchtipp: »Das kurze Leben« von Juan Carlos Onetti

Dîner dans la pampa

En Uruguay, des pans importants de la vie sociale se jouent en fait sur le littoral. Quand on voyage dans l'arrière-pays, on se retrouve vite encerclé par la nature sauvage et une immense solitude. C'est dans cet environnement sauvage, dans le décor archaïque d'une ville laissée à l'abandon qu'en 2004 le chef étoilé argentin Francis Mallmann a transformé un ancien magasin en auberge. Loin du tumulte touristique, ce chef excentrique a trouvé l'ambiance parfaite pour ses expériences culinaires, notamment la cuisson au feu de bois et sur un gril spécial surdimensionné. Cet endroit reculé est ainsi devenu peu à peu un lieu de pèlerinage pour gourmets téméraires et pour tous ceux qui veulent passer quelques jours magiques au beau milieu de nulle part. Et ils sont légion car quand on goûte à l'excellente cuisine de Francis Mallmann, on désire renouveler l'expérience. C'est désormais possible grâce aux quelques chambres d'hôtel que ce visionnaire a aménagées lui-même dans un style rustique teinté de bohème-chic. À la réservation, le maître des lieux met d'ailleurs malicieusement en garde : « No shopping ! No nothing ! ». Garzón demeure en effet irrévocablement une ville fantôme et, en dehors de la découverte de la nature, les seules distractions possibles sont la baignade en piscine et la lecture dans une jolie bibliothèque. Le petit-déjeuner se prend dans la cour intérieure ombragée de l'hacienda, au cœur du pays gaucho, avec le beuglement des vaches et le chant des coqs en fond sonore. On ne saurait imaginer plus grande détente. Ici, c'est dans les assiettes qu'a lieu le spectacle.
Livre à emporter : « La Vie brève » de Juan Carlos Onetti

ANREISE	Nordöstlich von Punta del Este, 40 Kilometer von José Ignacio entfernt gelegen. Der nächste Flughafen ist der 74 Kilometer entfernte Aeropuerto de Punta del Este
PREIS	$$$$
ZIMMER	5 Zimmer, alle mit eleganten Bädern in Schwarz
KÜCHE	Mallmann kocht nach der alten Anden-Technik »infiernillo« (kleine Hölle) über Holzfeuer. Die Speisen werden auf heißen Eisengittern zum Tisch gebracht
GESCHICHTE	Im Zuge einer Immobilienkrise kaufte Mallmann kurzerhand das halbe Dorf Garzón und machte es im Jahr 2004 zum Mittelpunkt seines Kochuniversums
X-FAKTOR	Ein Pool unter Palmen, mitten im Nirgendwo

ACCÈS	Situé dans l'arrière-pays, au nord de Punta del Este, à 40 kilomètres de José Ignacio. L'aéroport le plus proche est celui de Punta del Este, à 74 kilomètres
PRIX	$$$$
CHAMBRES	5 chambres, toutes équipées d'élégantes salles de bain où domine le noir
RESTAURATION	Mallmann pratique la cuisson au feu de bois selon la technique andine ancienne infiernillo (petit enfer)
HISTOIRE	À la faveur d'une crise de l'immobilier, Mallmann a acheté tout de go la moitié de la localité de Garzón et en a fait le nombril de son univers culinaire en 2004
LES « PLUS »	La piscine sous les palmiers, au milieu de nulle part

Views of endless blue...
La Posada del Faro, Maldonado

La Posada del Faro, Maldonado

Views of endless blue

East of Montevideo and Punta del Este lies the vacation capital of Uruguay: white sandy beaches lapped by the waves of the Atlantic and the River Plate, and small townships with all the necessary infrastructure of shops, restaurants, and clubs. Many are overrun in the high season – but one place that has so far remained relatively quiet is José Ignacio, about 30 kilometres or just under 20 miles from Punta del Este. The perfect retreat for a summer vacation is the Posada del Faro, with its gleaming white walls, awnings, and sun umbrellas. It's just 30 metres (100 feet) from the ocean, and the views it commands of the Atlantic would be fit for the cinema. The pool is the purest blue, and so (most days) is the sky; and if that's not enough blue for you, there are blue-painted doors or blue carpets here and there around the interior. Otherwise the ten rooms are cream-coloured, with a good deal of wood; every room is individually furnished, but they all have their own secluded terrace with recliners or hammocks. In the evenings when the barbecue is fired up for the typical "asado" and diners take their places at long tables, it's like eating with good friends. The Posada del Faro is an excellent base for local excursions – to bathing resorts such as Punta del Este or La Paloma, to the Isla de Lobos with its colony of sea lions, or to Cerro Catedral, which at 513 metres (just under 1,600 feet) is Uruguay's loftiest peak!

Book to pack: "Blood Pact & Other Stories" by Mario Benedetti

La Posada del Faro
Calle de la Bahia esquina Timonel
Faro de José Ignacio
Maldonado
Uruguay
Tel: + 598 (44) 862 110
Fax: + 598 (44) 862 111
E-mail: contact@posadadelfaro.com
Website: www.posadadelfaro.com

DIRECTIONS	Situated 30 km/19 miles northeast of Punta del Este, on the Atlantic coast
RATES	$$
ROOMS	10 individually furnished double rooms
FOOD	A small barbecue restaurant with a fine view of the ocean
HISTORY	A new retreat, alongside an old lighthouse dating from 1877
X-FACTOR	Like a private villa far from the madding crowd

Schöne Aussichten

Östlich von Montevideo und Punta del Este liegen Uruguays Urlaubsparadiese: weiße Sandstrände, an die die Wellen von Río de la Plata und Atlantik rollen, sowie kleine Orte mit der nötigen Infrastuktur aus Geschäften, Restaurants und Clubs. Viele sind während der Hochsaison überlaufen – zu den noch relativ ruhigen Zielen gehört José Ignacio, rund 30 Kilometer von Punta del Este entfernt. Hier verbringt man die schönste Sommerfrische in der Posada del Faro, die mit ihren strahlend weißen Mauern, Sonnensegeln und Sonnenschirmen gerade einmal 30 Meter vom Meer entfernt steht und kinotaugliche Atlantikansichten möglich macht. Ganz in Blau zeigen sich auch der Pool und (an den meisten Tagen) der Himmel; und wer von diesen Farbtönen nicht genug bekommt, findet auch im Haus die ein oder andere blau gestrichene Tür oder einen blauen Teppich. Ansonsten herrschen in den zehn Zimmern Cremetöne und viel Holz vor; jeder Raum ist unterschiedlich eingerichtet, aber alle besitzen eine eigene und geschützte Terrasse mit Liegestühlen oder Hängematten. Wie zu Gast bei guten Freunden fühlt man sich, wenn abends der Grill fürs typische »asado« angeheizt und an langen Tischen getafelt wird. Die Posada del Faro ist zudem ein guter Ausgangspunkt für Ausflüge – sei es in Badeorte wie Punta del Este oder La Paloma, zur Isla de Lobos mit ihrer Seelöwenkolonie oder auf den Cerro Catedral, mit 513 Metern der höchste Berg Uruguays!
Buchtipp: »Das Mädchen und der Feigenbaum« von Mario Benedetti

Une vue imprenable

Les paradis touristiques uruguayens se déploient à l'est de Montevideo et Punta del Este. Ici, on voit des plages de sable blanc sur lesquelles viennent rouler les vagues du Rio de La Plata et de l'Atlantique, des petits villages dotés du nécessaire : magasins, restaurants et clubs. Quand la saison bat son plein, les touristes sont souvent très nombreux, mais il y a des exceptions : José Ignacio, à une trentaine de kilomètres de Punta del Este, est un endroit relativement paisible. On peut passer un été merveilleux à la Posada del Faro qui se dresse avec ses murs d'un blanc éclatant, ses voilages pare-soleil et ses parasols juste à trente mètres de l'océan – un panorama à couper le souffle. La piscine et le ciel (la plupart du temps) sont également voués au bleu, et l'intérieur de la maison réserve aussi des accents de cette couleur apaisante ici et là, sur les portes ou les tapis de sol. Sinon des tons de crème et de bois naturel dominent dans les dix chambres. Chaque pièce est aménagée de manière individuelle mais toutes possèdent une terrasse protégée des regards et équipée de chaises longues ou de hamacs. Le soir tombé, lorsque le barbecue est allumé pour préparer l'« asado » typique et que les couverts sont disposés sur de longues tables, on a l'impression d'être chez des amis. En outre, la Posada del Faro est un bon point de départ pour les randonneurs, qu'ils désirent visiter les stations balnéaires de Punta del Este ou La Paloma, l'Isla de Lobos avec sa colonie de lions de mer ou le Cerro Catedral – le plus haut sommet d'Uruguay avec ses 513 mètres !
Livre à emporter : « La trêve » de Mario Benedetti

ANREISE	30 Kilometer nordöstlich von Punta del Este gelegen, direkt an der Atlantikküste
PREIS	$$
ZIMMER	10 individuell eingerichtete Doppelzimmer
KÜCHE	Kleines Grillrestaurant mit schöner Sicht aufs Meer
GESCHICHTE	Neue Adresse neben dem alten Leuchtturm anno 1877
X-FAKTOR	Wie eine private Villa abseits des Trubels

ACCÈS	Situé à 30 kilomètres au nord-est de Punta del Este, face à l'Atlantique
PRIX	$$
CHAMBRES	10 chambres doubles aménagées individuellement
RESTAURATION	Un petit restaurant de grillades avec une belle vue sur la mer
HISTOIRE	Une nouvelle adresse à côté du vieux phare datant de 1877
LES « PLUS »	Comme une villa particulière, loin des bruits de la ville

Retro style and patina...
Casa Zinc Posada, Punta del Este

Casa Zinc Posada, Punta del Este

Retro style and patina

What antique dealer Aaron Hojman actually wanted was simply to open a new exhibition space for his finest items. But things turned out differently, and his project ultimately resulted in the opening of an extremely loveable vintage hotel. Of course, in consequence Casa Zinc Posada is today adorned with hand-picked antiques from the threshold to the nightstand. There are six rooms, each a world of its own. Guests would search in vain here for the usual standards of luxury in furnishings. Instead, every square metre is occupied by lovingly chosen antiques, recycled materials and vintage items. For example, there is a library room, a classic school dormitory room and an old-fashioned architect's atelier. Those who appreciate retro style and lots of wonderful patina have found their hotel! From outside Casa Zinc exudes a somewhat austere industrial charm, but to walk into the courtyard is to enter the charming bohemian world of Aaron Hojman – and a zinc bath has been placed here. The operation of the hotel runs in a decidedly intimate and laid-back manner: guests dine at a communal table, and breakfast is served until late afternoon. Those who want to cook their own dinner can walk into the kitchen and prepare it for themselves. This likeable blend of the exclusive and the casual has made the hotel one of the hippest places in Uruguay, just a few minutes from the busy beach of Punta del Este – but somehow in a completely different place.

Book to pack: "The Truce" by Mario Benedetti

Casa Zinc Posada

La Barra, Punta del Este

Uruguay

Tel: + 598 (996) 200 66/(427) 730 03

E-mail: posada@casazinc.com

casazinc@gmail.com

Website: www.casazinc.com

DIRECTIONS	In the former fishing village of La Barra, 25 minutes from Punta del Este Airport
RATES	$$
ROOMS	6 individual rooms
FOOD	The legendary breakfast is served until four o'clock in the afternoon
HISTORY	In late 2008 a showroom was planned in the building – but the unintended result is a hotel
X-FACTOR	On the idyllic patio is a remarkable sight: a four-ton olive tree that came from an old estancia

Retro-Style und Patina

Eigentlich wollte der Antiquitätenhändler Aaron Hojman nur einen neuen Ausstellungsraum für seine schönsten Stücke aufmachen. Doch es kam etwas anders, sein Vorhaben endete letztlich in der Eröffnung eines überaus liebenswerten Vintage-Hotels. Folglich ist die Casa Zinc Posada heute natürlich von der Türschwelle bis zum Nachtkästchen mit handverlesenen Stücken dekoriert. Sechs Zimmer gibt es, und jedes ist eine eigene Welt, die üblichen Luxusstandards bei der Möblierung sucht man hier vergebens. Stattdessen finden sich auf jedem Meter liebevoll ausgewählte Antiquitäten, recycelte Materialien und Vintage-Stücke. Es gibt zum Beispiel ein Bibliothekszimmer, einen klassischen Schulschlafraum oder ein nostalgisches Architektenatelier. Wer auf Retro-Style und viel herrliche Patina steht, hat hier sein Hotel gefunden! Von außen verströmt die Casa Zinc noch einen eher herben Industriecharme, aber mit dem Innenhof betritt man dann die charmante Bohemewelt des Herrn Hojman – hier steht auch eine Zinkbadewanne. Der Hotelbetrieb wird dann auch betont familiär und lässig abgewickelt: Man sitzt an einem gemeinsamen Esstisch, und Frühstück gibt es bis spät in den Nachmittag hinein. Wer will, kann sich dann auch gleich selbst in die Küche stellen und sein Abendessen zubereiten. Die sympathische Mischung aus exklusiv und ungezwungen hat das Hotel zu einem der hippsten Plätze Uruguays gemacht, nur wenige Minuten vom quirligen Strand von Punta del Este entfernt – und doch irgendwie ganz woanders.

Buchtipp: »Die Gnadenfrist« von Mario Benedetti

Style rétro et patine

À l'origine, l'antiquaire Aaron Hojman voulait juste créer un nouveau show-room pour y exposer ses plus belles pièces. Mais les choses se sont passées un peu différemment, et il en est venu à ouvrir un hôtel vintage absolument charmant, la Casa Zinc, qui est bien sûr décoré jusque dans ses moindres recoins de pièces uniques. Chacune des six chambres est un univers en soi. N'y cherchez pas le luxe habituel en matière d'aménagement intérieur. En revanche, le moindre mètre carré est investi par des antiquités choisies avec amour, des matériaux recyclés ou des objets vintage, qui recréent l'ambiance, par exemple, d'une bibliothèque, d'une salle de classe-dortoir ou d'un atelier d'architecte à l'ancienne. Amateurs de style rétro et de superbe patine à foison, voilà un hôtel pour vous ! Le charme industriel plutôt froid de l'extérieur cède la place, dès le seuil du patio, au charmant univers bohème de Monsieur Hojman – il y a même une baignoire en zinc ! Convivialité et décontraction sont la philosophie affichée par la maison : on prend ses repas à la table commune, et le petit-déjeuner est servi jusqu'en milieu d'après-midi. Le soir, la cuisine est même à la disposition des hôtes. Ce mélange sympathique de haut de gamme et de décontraction a fait de cet établissement l'un des endroits les plus branchés d'Uruguay, à deux pas de la plage animée de Punta del Este, mais dont il semble être pour ainsi dire à des années-lumière.

Livre à emporter : « La Trêve » de Mario Benedetti

ANREISE	Im ehemaligen Fischerdorf La Barra gelegen, 25 Minuten vom Flughafen Punta del Este entfernt
PREIS	$$
ZIMMER	6 individuelle Zimmer
KÜCHE	Das legendäre Frühstück wird bis vier Uhr nachmittags serviert
GESCHICHTE	Ende 2008 wurde in dem Gebäude ein Showroom geplant – entstanden ist versehentlich ein Hotel
X-FAKTOR	Der idyllische Patio bietet eine besondere Sehenswürdigkeit: einen vier Tonnen schweren Olivenbaum, der von einer alten Estancia stammt

ACCÈS	Dans l'ancien village de pêcheurs La Barra, à 25 minutes de l'aéroport de Punte del Este
PRIX	$$
CHAMBRES	6 chambres ayant chacune un cachet particulier
RESTAURATION	Le petit-déjeuner légendaire est servi jusqu'à 16 heures
HISTOIRE	Le show-room prévu au départ, en 2008, a pris une tournure inattendue : on a en fait créé un hôtel
LES « PLUS »	Le patio idyllique abrite une vraie curiosité : un olivier de quatre tonnes, qui provient d'une ancienne estancia

Following nature's trail...
Yacutinga Lodge, Misiones

Yacutinga Lodge, Misiones

Following nature's trail

There are times when you long for the fantastic world of story-book adventures, that world of pursuits through the undergrowth of deep forests, with precarious suspended bridges spanning daunting chasms, leaves the size of surfboards meeting to roof the path with green, and toast roasted at the open campfire. The place to satisfy the craving is the Yacutinga Lodge, tucked away in the jungle borderlands between Argentina and Brazil, 80 kilometres (49 miles) from the famous Iguazú Falls. The buildings, made of local stone and thick wooden planks, mantled softly in green and appointed with organically-shaped furniture and with fabrics in muted hues, were designed to harmonise with the enchanting natural setting. Created by its owner Carlos Sandoval and built with local people, Yacutinga is an all-round environmental venture, and offers ecotourism complete with every comfort – guests live not just *in* but *with* nature. The Lodge nestles in a 570-hectare private reserve, which in turn is part of a 270,000-hectare conservation area – in contrast to much of the region, no forest clearing is permitted here. More than 2,000 plant species and some 400 species of animals benefit from this. To walk through the forest is to feel you're in some vast Jungle Book, with butterflies, snakes, monkeys, and birds waiting to be discovered. Professional guides accompany all excursions, on foot or by boat, or indeed at night, when the sounds and smells are muted and lend the forest a very special magic. It's worth planning at least three days at the Lodge, but most guests stay much longer anyway – because Yacutinga does have this in common with the adventure story realm: once you're there, you'll never want to leave.

Book to pack: "Concerning the Angels" by Rafael Alberti

Yacutinga Lodge	
Lote 7a	
3371 Almte, Brown	
Misiones	
Argentina	
Tel: + 54 (911) 4099 0057	
E-mail: yacutinga@yacutinga.com	
Website: www.yacutinga.com	

DIRECTIONS	Situated in the far northeast of Argentina, 80 km/49 miles from Iguazú. Transfer from Puerto Iguazu (Argentina) is organised
RATES	$$$$
ROOMS	6 double rooms, 14 three-bed rooms and 1 special suite
FOOD	Gourmet local cusine, fresh produce grown in the Lodge's own kitchen gardens. Open-air barbecues
HISTORY	Conceived as a dream sustainable dream destination for eco-tourists
X-FACTOR	A green thought in a green shade

Der Natur auf der Spur

Manchmal wünscht man sich ja auf diese fantastischen Abenteuerspielplätze zurück: Wo man im tiefsten Wald durchs Gebüsch pirschte und auf Hängebrücken gefährlich aussehende Schluchten überquerte, wo Blätter so groß wie Surfbretter grüne Dächer über den Wegen bildeten und wo am offenen Feuer Stockbrot geröstet werden konnte. Diese Sehnsucht kann gestillt werden – mit einer Reise zur Yacutinga Lodge, die sich im Dschungel an der Grenze zwischen Argentinien und Brasilien, 80 Kilometer von den berühmten Iguazú-Wasserfällen entfernt, versteckt. In Harmonie mit der verwunschenen Natur wurden hier Häuser aus einheimischem Stein und dicken Holzplanken gebaut, jedes von Grün umhüllt wie von einem weichen Mantel und mit organisch geformten Möbeln sowie Stoffen in weichen Tönen ausgestattet. Yacutinga, das von dem Besitzer Carlos Sandoval konzipiert und mit lokalen Arbeitern errichtet wurde, ist ein umfassendes Umweltprojekt und verspricht komfortablen Ökotourismus – es lässt seine Gäste nicht nur in der Natur, sondern mit der Natur leben. Die Lodge liegt in einem 570 Hektar großen Privatreservat, das zur Lodge gehört und das wiederum Teil eines 270.000 Hektar großen Schutzgebietes ist – hier darf im Gegensatz zu weiten Teilen der Region nicht gerodet werden. Mehr als 2.000 verschiedene Pflanzen- und rund 400 Tierarten profitieren davon; wer durch den Wald wandert, fühlt sich wie in einem überdimensionalen Dschungelbuch, entdeckt Schmetterlinge, Schlangen, Affen und Vögel. Professionelle Führer begleiten jede Exkursion – sei es zu Fuß, per Boot oder sogar während der Nacht, wenn die Geräusche und Gerüche weicher werden und dem Wald einen ganz besonderen Zauber verleihen. Mindestens drei Tage sollte man sich für die Lodge Zeit nehmen, doch die meisten Gäste bleiben ohnehin viel länger – denn auch darin ähneln sich ein Abenteuerspielplatz und Yacutinga: Ist man einmal dort, will man nie wieder weg.

Buchtipp: »Die Engel« von Rafael Alberti

Vacances vertes

Parfois on se surprend à avoir la nostalgie de ces fantastiques terrains de jeux d'aventure : on se faufilait courageusement dans les taillis épais, on traversait des gorges dangereuses sur des ponts suspendus ; d'immenses feuilles vertes recouvraient les sentiers et on pouvait faire griller du pain sec sur des feux de camp. On peut retrouver tout cela au Yacutinga Lodge qui se dissimule dans la jungle à la frontière argentino-brésilienne, à 80 kilomètres des célèbres chutes d'Iguazú. En harmonie avec la nature, les quatre habitations construites ici avec la pierre locale et des planches épaisses, sont habillées de verdure et abritent des meubles aux formes organiques et des étoffes aux teintes pastel. Yacutinga, conçu par son propriétaire Carlos Sandoval et bâti par des architectes locaux, est un projet écologique de vaste envergure et offre un refuge confortable aux adeptes du tourisme vert – les hôtes ne vivent pas seulement dans la nature, ils vivent avec la nature. Le Lodge se trouve dans une réserve naturelle privée de 570 hectares, elle-même faisant partie d'un territoire protégé de 270 000 hectares dans lequel il est interdit de déboiser, contrairement à ce qui se passe dans de vastes zones de la région. Plus de 2 000 espèces végétales et environ 400 espèces animales vivent ici : celui qui se balade en forêt découvre des papillons, des serpents, des singes et des oiseaux. Des guides professionnels accompagnent toutes les excursions, qu'elles se fassent à pied, en bateau, ou la nuit quand les animaux sont actifs, quand les bruits et les odeurs se font plus lourds et donnent à la forêt un charme particulier. Il est recommandé de rester au moins trois jours au Lodge, mais la plupart des hôtes y séjournent beaucoup plus longtemps. C'est aussi le point commun entre Yacutinga et le terrain de jeux d'aventure – une fois que l'on y a pris goût, on ne veut plus le quitter.

Livre à emporter : « Marin à terre » de Rafael Alberti

ANREISE	Im äußersten Nordosten Argentiniens gelegen, 80 Kilometer von Iguazú entfernt. Transfer ab Puerto Iguazú (Argentinen) wird organisiert
PREIS	$$$$
ZIMMER	6 Doppelzimmer, 14 Dreibettzimmer, 1 Spezialsuite
KÜCHE	Lokale Gourmetküche, frische Produkte aus eigenem Anbau, Barbecues unter freiem Himmel
GESCHICHTE	Als Traumziel für Ökotouristen konzipiert
X-FAKTOR	Alles im grünen Bereich

ACCÈS	Situé à l'extrême nord-est de l'Argentine, à 80 kilomètres d'Iguazú. Transfert organisé à partir d'Iguazú (Argentine)
PRIX	$$$$
CHAMBRES	6 chambres doubles, 14 chambres à trois lits
RESTAURATION	Cuisine gastronomique locale, produits frais cultivés sur place, barbecues en plein air
HISTOIRE	Pour les touristes respectueux de l'environnement
LES « PLUS »	Des vacances vertes

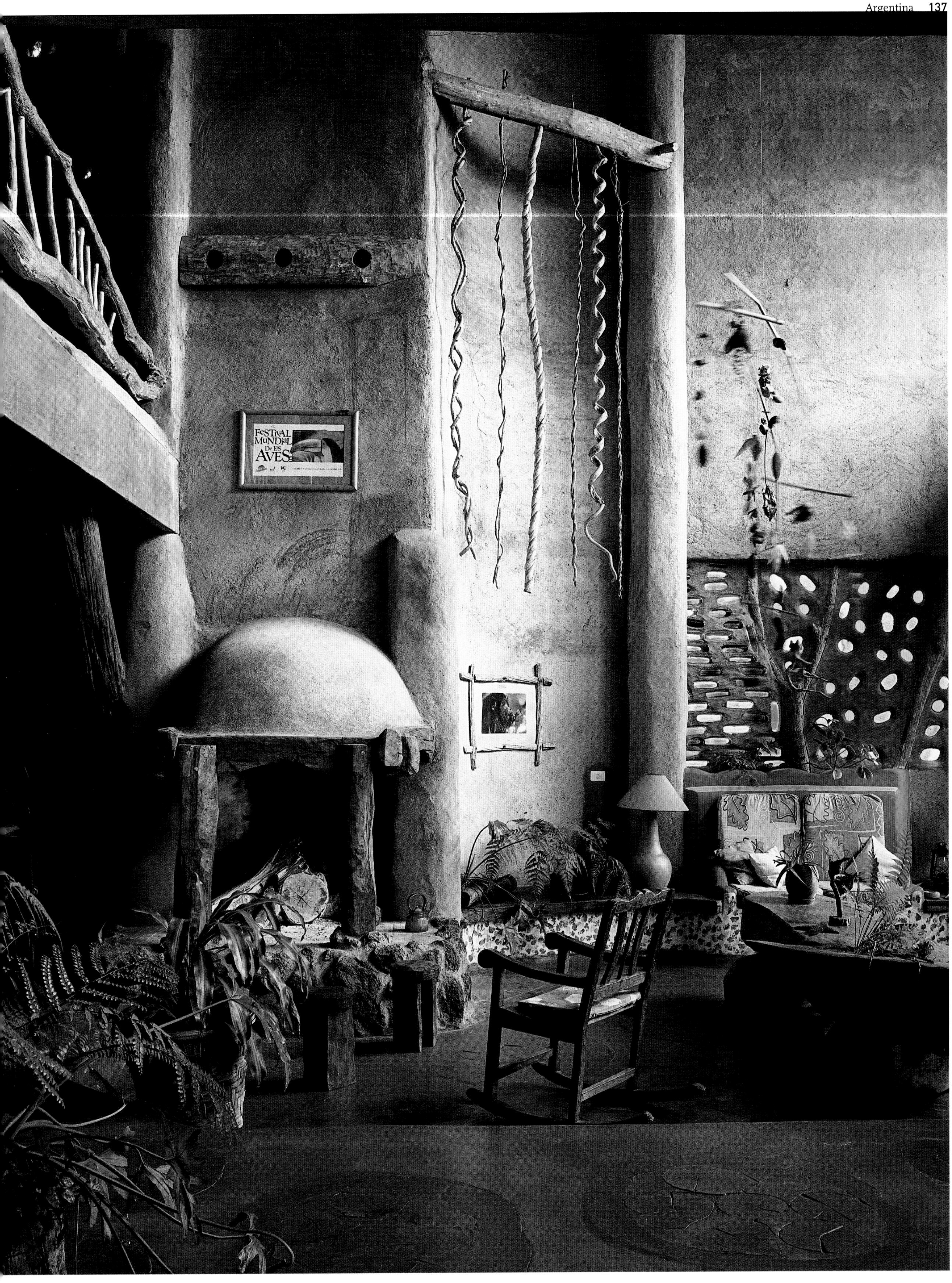
FESTIVAL
MUNDIAL
DE LAS
AVES

A jungle lodge...
Posada La Bonita, Misiones

Posada La Bonita, Misiones

A jungle lodge

This jungle is more like an enchanted forest in a fairy tale. The green of the twined plants is so rich you almost think it's dripping from the leaves. A faint veil seems always to be drifting upon the air, and a tremendous waterfall is tumbling into the depths. Never has it been so easy to achieve a state resembling that of meditation – the Posada La Bonita grants the soul the very best, from the very first moment. A jungle lodge in the extreme northeast of Argentina, it is entirely one with its natural setting. The rooms are done in an abundance of wood and hand-woven fabrics, and with greenery visible from every room and veranda you won't miss the high-tech environment of the world you've left behind for a single second. The perfect day in La Bonita begins with the dawn chorus and breakfast in the open, and then it's time to explore the labyrinthine river system and forests in a kayak or hand-carved canoe, or get to know the country on horseback. After a candlelit dinner with lounge music in the background you can idle for a while in a hammock before turning in – no need to worry about mosquitoes, since they rarely make an appearance at this altitude. At this hour, the soothing splash of the waterfall is better than any sleeping pill. And if you find the sheer fascination of water is getting to you, try visiting the nearby Saltos del Moconá, where the Uruguay River races down three kilometres (1.8 miles) of breathtaking cascades.

Book to pack: "What the Night Tells the Day" by Hector Bianciotti

Posada La Bonita	
Moconá, El Soberbio	
Misiones	
Argentina	
Tel: + 54 (911) 5842 8386	
E-mail: info@posadalabonita.net	
Website: www.posadalabonita.com.ar	

DIRECTIONS	Situated 300 km/188 miles southeast of Iguazú airport. The transfer is organised
RATES	$
ROOMS	6 double rooms
FOOD	Regional and Italian cuisine, with a substantial range of vegetarian fare
HISTORY	Opened in March 1999
X-FACTOR	The full glorious spectacle of nature

Dschungellodge

Dieser Urwald ist ein Märchenwald: Die ineinander verschlungenen Pflanzen sind so sattgrün, dass man glaubt, die
Farbe von den Blättern tropfen zu sehen, in der Luft scheint
immer ein leichter Schleier zu schweben, und ein mächtiger
Wasserfall stürzt in die Tiefe. Nie war es so einfach, sich in
einen meditationsähnlichen Zustand zu versetzen – wer in
die Posada La Bonita zieht, gönnt seiner Seele vom ersten
Moment an nur das Beste. Die Dschungellodge im äußersten Nordosten Argentiniens ist mit der Natur verwachsen,
hier wohnt man in mit viel Holz und handgewebten Stoffen
ausgestatteten Zimmern, blickt von jedem Raum und jeder
Veranda aus ins Grüne und vermisst die High-Tech-Errungenschaften der restlichen Welt keine Sekunde lang. Der perfekte Tag in La Bonita beginnt mit einem Konzert der Vögel
und einem Frühstück im Freien, anschließend spürt man
vom Kajak oder handgeschnitzten Kanu aus die Geheimnisse der Flusslabyrinthe und des Waldes auf oder entdeckt die
Umgebung per Pferd. Nach einem Abendessen bei Kerzenschein und mit Loungemusik im Hintergrund schaukelt
man in der Hängematte der Nacht entgegen und muss sich
dabei nicht vor Mückenstichen fürchten – dank der Höhenlage kommen die angriffslustigen Insekten hier so gut wie
gar nicht vor. Das Plätschern des Wasserfalls wirkt zu später
Stunde dann besser als jede Baldriantablette – wen während
des Urlaubs die Faszination des nassen Elements nicht mehr
loslässt, der sollte auch zu den nahen Saltos del Moconá fahren, wo der Fluss Uruguay auf einer Länge von drei Kilometern eine rauschende Kaskade bildet.
**Buchtipp: »Wie die Spur des Vogels in der Luft« von
Hector Bianciotti**

Lodge de la jungle

Cette forêt semble sortie tout droit d'un conte de fées : les
plantes qui s'entrelacent sont d'un vert si intense que l'on
croit voir la couleur goutter de leurs feuilles, un voile léger
de condensation flotte dans l'air et une imposante cascade se
jette dans les profondeurs. Jamais il n'a été aussi facile qu'ici
de se retrouver dans un état proche de la méditation – celui
qui réside à la Posada La Bonita peut choyer son âme dès le
premier moment. Situé à l'extrême nord-est de l'Argentine, ce
lodge est intimement lié à la nature environnante. Le bois et
les étoffes tissées à la main abondent dans les chambres qui
offrent toutes, ainsi que les vérandas, une vue sur la verdure.
Ici, on ne regrette pas une seconde les progrès technologiques du reste du monde. À La Bonita, la journée commence
avec le chant des oiseaux au réveil et un petit-déjeuner en
plein air. Ensuite, on part en kayak ou dans un canoë sculpté
à la main, à la découverte des mystères du fleuve et de la forêt
ou bien on fait une randonnée à cheval. Après un dîner aux
chandelles avec une musique douce en fond sonore, on peut
savourer la tombée de la nuit dans un hamac. Nulle crainte
à avoir des moustiques, il n'y en a pratiquement pas à cette
altitude. Le murmure au loin de la cascade fait plus d'effet
que n'importe quelle pilule pour dormir. Et si pendant ces vacances, la fascination de l'eau ne vous quitte plus, allez donc
visiter les chutes Saltos del Moconá, là où le fleuve Uruguay
forme sur trois kilomètres une cascade impressionnante.
**Livre à emporter : « Comme la trace de l'oiseau dans l'air » de
Hector Bianciotti**

ANREISE	300 Kilometer südöstlich des Flughafens Iguazú gelegen. Transfer wird organisiert
PREIS	$
ZIMMER	6 Doppelzimmer
KÜCHE	Regionale und italienische Menüs, großes Angebot für Vegetarier
GESCHICHTE	Im März 1999 eröffnet
X-FAKTOR	Ein Naturschauspiel

ACCÈS	Situé à 300 kilomètres au sud-est de l'aéroport d'Iguazú. Le transfert est organisé
PRIX	$
CHAMBRES	6 chambres doubles
RESTAURATION	Menus régionaux et italiens. Grand choix de plats végétariens
HISTOIRE	Ouvert depuis mars 1999
LES « PLUS »	Un spectacle de la nature

Homage to fine wine...

Bodega El Esteco de Cafayate, Salta

Bodega El Esteco de Cafayate, Salta

Homage to fine wine

It's almost like being in the old heart of a Spanish town. Through the imposing arched gateways you come upon whitewashed buildings with rounded arches, bell towers and patios, with geraniums and roses to fill the scene with colour and fragrance. And that first impression is absolutely right: the colonial-inspired architecture of the Bodega El Esteco de Cafayate was modelled on the Barrio de la Santa Cruz, the historic centre of Seville. Still, the surroundings quickly remind you that you're in South America. All around the estate are vineyards, stretching as far as the horizon, it seems, or at least to the Andean Cordilleras. The grapes that grow in the Valles Calchaquíes are first class, thanks to the 340 days of sunshine per annum, the cool nights, and an ideal high-lying location some 1,800 metres (about 5,900 feet) above sea level – and the local wine-growers export their vintages all over the world. The Bodega El Esteco de Cafayate (hitherto also known to aficionados as the Bodega La Rosa) was established in 1892 by two brothers, David and Salvador Michel, who hailed from France. Currently it is being re-structured as a kind of boutique winery: only choice wines will be produced in the future, bearing names such as "Don David" or "Altimus". This exclusivity is the hallmark of the country hotel as well. Offering the authentic experience of the vintner's way of life on a private farmhouse, without losing out on any of the comforts and amenities of a modern hotel. The plan even envisages Argentina's first wine spa, where the active ingredients of grapes are harnessed to a wellness regime. The leisure programme includes vineyard tours, photo expeditions, riding, trekking, and fishing trips. Regardless of which programme you opt for, the finest hours may well be those that begin at sunset, when real country cooking is served in the inviting dining rooms – with the estate's own fine wines.

Book to pack: "Imagining Argentina" by Lawrence Thornton

Bodega El Esteco de Cafayate
Ruta Nacional 40 and Ruta Nacional 68
4427 Cafayate
Salta
Argentina
Tel: + 54 (3868) 422 229 and 421 753
E-mail: reservas@patiosdecafayate.com
Website: www.patiosdecafayate.com

DIRECTIONS	Situated 120 km/75 miles (two and a half hours by road) south of Salta
RATES	$$
ROOMS	32 rooms and suites
FOOD	Argentine country food, with first-class wines
HISTORY	A 19th-century winery with recently added guest-house accommodation
X-FACTOR	In vino veritas

Dem Wein gewidmet

Man könnte meinen, in einer spanischen Altstadt zu sein: Hinter mächtigen Torbögen liegen weiß getünchte Gebäude mit Rundbögen, Glockentürmen und Patios, in denen Geranien oder Rosen für süßen Duft und Farbe sorgen. Und wirklich ist die kolonial angehauchte Architektur der Bodega El Esteco de Cafayate dem Barrio de la Santa Cruz, dem historischen Zentrum Sevillas, nachempfunden – doch das Umland holt einen schnell nach Südamerika zurück. Rings um das Anwesen dehnt sich ein Weinanbaugebiet aus, das bis zum Horizont oder zumindest bis zu den Andenkordilleren im Hintergrund zu reichen scheint. Mehr als 340 Sonnentage, kühle Nächte und eine ideale Höhenlage von 1.800 Metern lassen in den Valles Calchaquíes erstklassige Trauben reifen – hier ansässige Winzer exportieren ihre Tropfen in alle Welt. Die Bodega El Esteco de Cafayate (Insidern war sie bislang auch als Bodega La Rosa bekannt) wurde 1892 von französischen Einwanderern, den Brüdern David und Salvador Michel, gegründet und wird derzeit zu einer Art »Boutique-Winery« umstrukturiert: Nur noch Spitzenweine mit klingenden Namen wie »Don David« oder »Altimus« sollen künftig produziert werden. Ebenso exklusiv geht es auch im angeschlossenen Landhotel zu. Hier soll man das Winzerleben wie in einem privaten Farmhaus erleben, ohne auf die Annehmlichkeiten eines modernen Hotels verzichten zu müssen. Geplant ist sogar das erste Wein-Spa Argentiniens, in dem die Wirkstoffe der Trauben für Wellness und Wohlbefinden genutzt werden. Auf dem Entspannungsprogramm stehen zudem Touren durch die Wineyards, Fotosafaris, Ausritte, Trekkings und Angelausflüge. Doch ganz egal, für welches Programm man sich entscheidet: Die vielleicht schönsten Stunden beginnen bei Sonnenuntergang, wenn in den gemütlichen Gutsräumen echte Landhausküche serviert wird – und dazu feine Weine aus eigenem Anbau im Glas glänzen.

Buchtipp: »Wiedersehen in Argentinien« von Hubert Landes

Le goût du vin

On se croirait dans une vieille cité espagnole : derrière de vastes portails s'élèvent des bâtiments blancs dotés d'arches en plein cintre, de clochers et de patios dans lesquels des géraniums ou des roses apportent des accents de couleur et des parfums suaves. L'architecture aux accents coloniaux de la Bodega El Esteco de Cafayate est réellement inspirée de celle du Barrio de la Santa Cruz, le cœur historique de Séville. Mais l'illusion se dissipe rapidement car, autour de la propriété, les vignobles semblent se déployer jusqu'à la cordillère des Andes. Avec plus de 340 journées d'ensoleillement, des nuits fraîches et une altitude de près de 1 800 mètres au-dessus du niveau de la mer, les Valles Calchaquies voient mûrir des raisins de premier choix – les viticulteurs de la région exportent leurs crus dans le monde entier. La Bodega El Esteco de Cafayate (jusqu'ici Bodega La Rosa pour les initiés), fondée en 1892 par des immigrés français, les frères David et Salvador Michel, est en cours de restructuration et ne produira bientôt plus que des vins exceptionnels au doux nom de « Don David » ou « Altimus ». L'hôtel annexe subit la même métamorphose luxueuse. Les hôtes doivent vivre ici comme dans un domaine viticole sans renoncer aux commodités d'un hôtel moderne. On envisage même la création du premier spa d'Argentine dans lequel les substances actives du raisin seront utilisées pour la remise en forme et le bien-être. Le programme-détente prévoit aussi des randonnées à travers la région viticole, des safaris photo, du trekking et des excursions de pêche. Mais les heures les plus douces seront sans doute celles que l'on passe après le coucher du soleil quand la bonne cuisine rustique est servie dans les salles accueillantes – sans oublier les vins délectables produits sur le terroir.

Livre à emporter : « La trame céleste » de Adolfo Bioy Casares

ANREISE	120 Kilometer (zweieinhalb Fahrtstunden) südlich von Salta gelegen
PREIS	$$
ZIMMER	32 Zimmer und Suiten
KÜCHE	Argentinische Landhausküche, erstklassige Weine
GESCHICHTE	Ein Weingut aus dem 19. Jahrhundert mit einem neu angebauten Gästehaus
X-FAKTOR	In vino veritas

ACCÈS	Situé à 20 kilomètres (deux heures et demie de voiture) au sud de Salta
PRIX	$$
CHAMBRES	32 chambres et suites
RESTAURATION	Cuisine de pays, vins de premier choix
HISTOIRE	Un domaine viticole du XIXᵉ siècle doté d'un hôtel récent
LES « PLUS »	In vino veritas

A remote world by the water.

Pirá Lodge, Corrientes Province

Pirá Lodge, Corrientes Province

A remote world by the water

It's called the tiger of the rivers – *salminus maxillosus*, with its shimmering yellow scales, razor-sharp teeth, and powerful fins, which enable it to glide through the water at an extraordinary speed. The best place to go in pursuit of this salmon-like fish is the swamplands of Iberá, a region of crystal-clear rivers and shallow inlets, virtually untouched by humankind and almost twice the size of Florida's Everglades. For anglers and fly fishermen, this part of northern Argentina is still an insider's tip – as is the Pirá Lodge, in Corrientes Province. It is not remotely what you would normally expect a fishermen's hotel to be: there are no fusty odours, no rods to trip over, and the accommodation doesn't consist of four-bed dorms. Here, a maximum of ten guests reside comfortably in five well-appointed double rooms. They're light and airy, the furniture is hand-crafted, and a bath with a view is included in the price. The Pirá Lodge is country style of a sophisticated order, complete with a 20-metre (66-feet) pool and a barbecue restaurant, well-trained staff, and an angling store on the hotel premises. The season runs from September to April; but the Pirá is open outside this period too, and affords visitors at all times the opportunity to explore the countryside on horseback or in a kayak – or simply to enjoy the sun.

Book to pack: "The House of Bernarda Alba" by Federico Garcia Lorca

Pirá Lodge	
c/o Nervous Waters	
Av. Figueroa Alcorta 3351 (Piso 2, oficina 228)	
Cod. postal 1425, Buenos Aires	
Argentina	
Tel: + 54 (11) 4801 1008	
E-mail: info@nervouswaters.com	
Website: www.nervouswaters.com	

DIRECTIONS	Situated 640 km/400 miles north of Buenos Aires. The flight to Resistencia or Corrientes costs US$ 360 per person. The transfer to the Lodge takes about four hours and is organised for guests
RATES	$$$
ROOMS	5 double rooms (each with en suite bath)
FOOD	Gourmet cuisine, à la carte menu
HISTORY	The first lodge to target for Golden Dorado
X-FACTOR	An active vacation in first-class fishing country

Ferne Welt am Wasser

Er gilt als der »Tiger der Flüsse« – der *Salminus Maxillosus* mit seinen gelb schimmernden Schuppen, seinen scharfen Zähnen und seinen starken Flossen, die ihn im Rekordtempo durchs Wasser gleiten lassen. Wer auf die Jagd nach diesem lachsähnlichen Fisch gehen möchte, tut dies am besten in den Sümpfen von Iberá, einem Marschland aus kristallklaren Flüssen und seichten Buchten, fast unberührt und fast zweieinhalbmal so groß wie die Everglades in Florida. Unter Sport- und Fliegenfischern gilt diese Region im Norden Argentiniens noch als Geheimtipp – genau wie die Pirá Lodge, die in der Provinz Corrientes ihre Pforten geöffnet hat. Sie ist weit entfernt von allem, was man sich im Allgemeinen unter einem Hotel für Angler vorstellt: Hier liegt kein modriger Geruch in der Luft, man stolpert nicht ständig über Ruten und schläft auch nicht in Vierbettzimmern – hier logieren maximal zehn Gäste in fünf komfortablen Doppelzimmern; viel Licht, handgefertigte Möbel und eine Badewanne mit Aussicht inbegriffen. Ganz im Sinne des gehobenen Countrystils gehören auch ein 20-Meter-Pool und ein Grillrestaurant zur Lodge, und die fischenden Gäste freuen sich über gut ausgebildetes Personal und einen hoteleigenen Anglershop. Saison ist hier von September bis April; doch Pirá hat auch außerhalb dieser Monate geöffnet und empfängt dann vor allem Besucher, die die umliegende Natur hoch zu Pferd oder im Kajak erkunden – oder einfach nur die Sonne genießen.

Buchtipp: »Bernarda Albas Haus« von Federico Garcia Lorca

Ici l'on pêche

Avec ses écailles aux reflets jaunes, ses dents acérées et ses nageoires puissantes qui lui permettent de glisser dans l'eau à toute allure, le dorado *Salminus Maxillosus* est le « tigre del rio ». Les amateurs peuvent pêcher ce poisson qui ressemble au saumon dans les marais d'Iberá, un delta de rivières cristallines et de baies peu profondes, pratiquement vierges et deux fois et demie plus vaste que les Everglades de Floride. Cette région du nord de l'Argentine n'est encore connue que de quelques clubs de pêche et de pêcheurs à la mouche – et c'est aussi le cas du Pirá Lodge qui a ouvert ses portes dans la province de Corrientes. Il ne ressemble pas à l'hôtel pour pêcheur tel qu'on l'imagine en général : ici pas d'odeur de vase, pas de cannes à pêche où l'on se prend sans cesse les pieds et pas de chambres à quatre lits. L'endroit peut loger dix personnes dans cinq chambres doubles confortables. La lumière abondante, des meubles fabriqués à la main et une baignoire avec vue sont compris dans la location. Tout à fait dans l'esprit du style Country élégant, une piscine de 20 mètres de long et un restaurant à grillades font également partie du Lodge, et les hôtes sont satisfaits du personnel aimable et compétent et de la boutique offrant des articles de pêche qui appartient à l'hôtel. La saison de la pêche débute au mois de septembre et s'achève en avril, mais Pirá est ouvert toute l'année et accueille surtout des visiteurs qui veulent explorer la nature environnante à cheval ou en kayak, ou simplement profiter du soleil.

Livre à emporter : « La maison de Bernarda Alba » de Federico Garcia Lorca

ANREISE	640 Kilometer nördlich von Buenos Aires gelegen. Flug nach Resistencia oder Corrientes US$ 360 pro Person. Rund vierstündige Weiterfahrt zur Lodge wird organisiert
PREIS	$$$
ZIMMER	5 Doppelzimmer. Mit je eigenem Bad
KÜCHE	Gourmetküche, à la carte
GESCHICHTE	Die erste Lodge, die sich dem Golden Dorado widmet
X-FAKTOR	Aktivurlaub in einem erstklassigen Anglerrevier

ACCÈS	Situé à 640 kilomètres au nord de Buenos Aires. Vols à destination de Resistencia ou Corrientes US$ 360 par personne. Le trajet de quatre heures jusqu'au Lodge est organisé
PRIX	$$$
CHAMBRES	5 chambres doubles (avec salle de bains)
RESTAURATION	Cuisine gastronomique à la carte
HISTOIRE	Le premier Lodge consacré au Golden Dorado
LES « PLUS »	Des vacances actives dans une zone de pêche de premier choix

Roaming further afield...
Dos Lunas, Province Córdoba

Dos Lunas, Province Córdoba

Roaming further afield

It was at Mount Colchequin that the indigenous Comechingones suffered their worst moment. Faced on this rocky terrain with defeat at the hands of the Spanish, they leapt from the peak to their deaths, preferring to die with pride rather than on Spanish pikes. Happily, this onetime battleground is now a peaceful place. To gaze across the green and gently undulating country of Ongamira, where weather-rounded rocks repose like slumbering creatures of fantasy with russet-brown backs, is to behold a soft and tranquil landscape. And it is here that we find the Dos Lunas country hotel, in the heart of 3,000 hectares of what seems utterly unspoilt nature. For new arrivals, the best way to acclimatise to the vast and peaceful spaces of Córdoba province is to relax by the pool in the garden; but no later than day two you should be out and about, exploring the region. Take a long walk through the forests and hills, for instance, forever moving on from one breathtaking lookout point to the next. Or if you want to roam further afield, Dos Lunas offers horse riding – from short canters, to excursions into the mountains, to trekking expeditions lasting days. If you opt for the long version, you'll spend your nights camping in the open, listening to the guides' tales and guitar playing by the campfire. If you're a little weary on your return, and your muscles are aching, Dos Lunas has all the creature comfort you need, and hot baths to relax in. The establishment is also celebrated for its country cooking – from breakfast with home-baked bread and honey from the region to barbecues by the pool, this is the taste of Argentina!

Book to pack: "Don Segundo Sombra" by Ricardo Güiraldes

Dos Lunas Horse Riding Lodge
Ruta provincial 17 s/n
Ongamira
Province Córdoba
Argentina
Tel: + 54 (911) 2637 5123
E-mail: doslunas@doslunas.com.ar
Website: www.doslunas.com.ar

DIRECTIONS	Situated 120 km/75 miles north of Córdoba (domestic flights from Buenos Aires), 90 minutes by road. The transfer costs US$ 140 each way
RATES	$$$
ROOMS	2 double rooms and 3 apartments for 3–5 guests
FOOD	Good, substantial fare, using regional produce
HISTORY	A modern country hotel on historic ground
X-FACTOR	Nature pure and simple – as far as the eye can see

Ein weites Feld

Am Berg Colchequin musste der Stamm der Comechingones einst seine größte Niederlage hinnehmen: Die Indianer drohten auf dem felsigen Gelände den Kampf gegen die Spanier zu verlieren und stürzten sich vom Gipfel in den Tod, um zumindest mit Stolz zu sterben und nicht durch spanische Speere. Der einstige Kampfplatz präsentiert sich heute zum Glück friedvoll: Wer über das leicht gewellte und grüne Land von Ongamira blickt, in dem rund geschliffene Felsen wie schlafende Fantasiewesen mit rotbraunen Rücken liegen, sieht eine sanfte und stille Landschaft. Hier steht auch das Landhotel Dos Lunas – inmitten von 3.000 Hektar wie unberührt wirkender Natur. Neuankömmlinge gewöhnen sich am besten am runden Pool im Garten an die Ruhe und Weitläufigkeit der Provinz Córdoba; doch spätestens am zweiten Tag sollte man die Region aktiv erkunden. Zum Beispiel bei einem langen Spaziergang durch die Wälder und Hügel und immer auf der Suche nach einem Aussichtspunkt, der noch schöner als der vorhergehende ist. Wen es noch weiter hinauszieht, für den bietet Dos Lunas Touren hoch zu Ross an – von kurzen Ausritten über Ausflüge in die Berge bis hin zu tagelangen Trekkings ist alles möglich. Wer sich für die Maxiversion entscheidet, campiert nachts im Freien, lauscht den Legenden der Guides und ihrem Gitarrenspiel am Lagerfeuer. Vielleicht schmerzen die Muskeln anschließend ein wenig, und vielleicht kommt man ein bisschen müde zurück; doch Dos Lunas sorgt mit gemütlichem Komfort und heißen Bädern für Entspannung. Berühmt ist das Haus auch für seine Landhausküche – vom Frühstück mit selbst gebackenem Brot und regionalem Honig bis hin zum Barbecue am Pool: So schmeckt Argentinien!

Buchtipp: »Das Buch vom Gaucho Sombra« von Ricardo Güiraldes

Les grands espaces

C'est sur la montagne de Colchequin que la tribu des Comechingones a subi l'une de ses plus terribles défaites. Alors qu'ils étaient sur le point d'être vaincus par les Espagnols, les Indiens préférèrent se jeter dans le vide plutôt que de se rendre. Ils voulaient mourir dans la dignité et non pas par les lances de leurs ennemis. L'ancien champ de bataille a retrouvé aujourd'hui un aspect serein. Légèrement vallonné, le territoire d'Ongamira se distingue par sa douceur et sa tranquillité, les rochers aux formes arrondies ressemblent à des êtres fabuleux assoupis dont on ne verrait que le dos rougeâtre. C'est ici qu'est situé également l'hôtel de campagne Dos Lunas – au milieu d'une nature de 3 000 hectares qui semble être restée intacte. Les nouveaux venus s'acclimateront au calme et à l'immensité de la province de Córdoba en se prélassant près de la piscine ronde dans le jardin. Mais après une journée de repos, nous leur recommandons de partir à la découverte de la région en faisant, par exemple, une longue promenade à travers les forêts et les collines, à la recherche des points de vue, tous plus beaux les uns que les autres. Pour celui qui désire s'aventurer plus loin, Dos Lunas propose des randonnées à cheval : petites virées dans les montagnes ou excursions de plusieurs jours, tout est possible. Si vous vous décidez pour la dernière solution, vous dormirez à la belle étoile, vous écouterez, allongé près du feu de camp, vos guides jouer de la guitare et vous conter les légendes du pays. Peut-être reviendrez-vous un peu fatigué et courbatu à Dos Lunas, mais avec son confort et ses bains chauds, l'hôtel vous invitera à la détente. Sa célèbre cuisine campagnarde vous redonnera aussi le punch nécessaire : petit déjeuner avec pain cuit maison et miel de la région, barbecue au bord de la piscine, c'est tout le goût de l'Argentine !

Livre à emporter : « Don Segundo Sombra » de Ricardo Güiraldes

ANREISE	120 Kilometer nördlich von Córdoba gelegen (dorthin Inlandsflüge ab Buenos Aires), Fahrtzeit 90 Minuten. Der Transfer kostet US$ 140 pro Strecke
PREIS	$$$
ZIMMER	2 Doppelzimmer und 3 Apartments für 3–5 Gäste
KÜCHE	Gut, kräftig und mit regionalen Produkten
GESCHICHTE	Modernes Landhotel auf geschichtsträchtigem Boden
X-FAKTOR	Natur pur – bis zum Horizont

ACCÈS	Situé à 120 kilomètres au nord de Córdoba (vols intérieurs depuis Buenos Aires), 90 minutes en voiture. Le transfert coûte US$ 140 par trajet
PRIX	$$$
CHAMBRES	2 chambres doubles et 3 appartements pour 3 à 5 personnes
RESTAURATION	Bonne cuisine rustique avec des produits régionaux
HISTOIRE	Hôtel de campagne sur un territoire chargé d'histoire
LES « PLUS »	De la nature à perte de vue

Staying with the President...

Estancia La Paz, Province Córdoba

Estancia La Paz, Province Córdoba

Staying with the President

"My political commitment never prevented me from maintaining a habit I was fond of. Every summer I spent at least two months in La Paz". The words are those of Julio Argentino Roca, President of Argentina from 1880 to 1886 and from 1898 to 1904 and a member of the "Generación del 80", a political/intellectual group that stood for immigration, economic growth, and a strong middle class. The gentlemen of the group debated their plans for reform not only in the capital, Buenos Aires, but also 110 kilometres (70 miles) away at Ascochinga, in the President's country house. For Julio Argentino Roca, La Paz was at once a private summer residence and a political meeting place – and the grand state style of that stance can still be sensed at the Estancia today. You reside in yellow-painted, lovingly restored buildings in the style of the colonial era or the Italian Renaissance, stroll in the vast and tranquil park laid out by French landscape architect Charles Thays, or take a dip in the pool, which at Roca's request was the first in the entire province to be of Olympic size. This is Argentine country life *de luxe* – naturally La Paz has two polo pitches as well, where national events take place, not to mention a first-rate 18-hole golf course, the grass on which looks so manicured that you picture the head greenkeeper personally trimming each blade of grass with nail clippers. And when it's time to adjourn to the nineteenth hole, if you're in luck the restaurant is serving the typical "cocina criolla" or there's a barbecue. Small wonder the master of the house used to feel a two-month summer break at La Paz was the absolute minimum.

Book to pack: "The Aleph" by Jorge Luis Borges

Estancia La Paz

Ruta E66, km 14

Province Córdoba

Argentina

Tel: + 54 (3525) 499 760 and (351) 152 727 867

E-mail: contacto@puebloestancialapaz.com

Website: www.puebloestancialapaz.com

DIRECTIONS	Situated 50 km/30 miles northeast of Córdoba airport (domestic flights from Buenos Aires)
RATES	$$–$$$
ROOMS	10 rooms
FOOD	Regional specialities (cocina criolla) and typical Argentine barbecue (asado)
HISTORY	What was once the President's country residence is now a luxurious country hotel
X-FACTOR	A summer break such as statesmen prefer

Zu Gast beim Präsidenten

»Mein politisches Engagement hat mich niemals von einer lieb gewonnenen Routine abgehalten: Ich verbrachte jeden Sommer mindestens zwei Monate in La Paz« – diese Zeilen stammen aus der Feder von Julio Argentino Roca, Argentiniens Präsident von 1880 bis 1886 sowie 1898 bis 1904 und Mitglied der politisch-intellektuellen Gruppe »Generación del 80«, die auf Einwanderung, Wirtschaftswachstum und einen starken Mittelstand setzte. Ihre Reformpläne diskutierten die Herren nicht nur in der Hauptstadt Buenos Aires, sondern auch im 110 Kilometer entfernten Ascochinga, im Landhaus des Präsidenten. La Paz war für Julio Argentino Roca privater Sommersitz und politischer Treffpunkt zugleich – und dieses staatstragende Flair verströmt die Estancia noch heute. Hier residiert man in gelb gestrichenen und liebevoll restaurierten Gebäuden im Stil der Kolonialzeit und der italienischen Renaissance, flaniert durch den weitläufigen und friedlichen Park, der die Handschrift des französischen Landschaftsarchitekten Charles Thays trägt, oder taucht im Pool unter, der auf Rocas Wunsch hin der erste mit olympischen Ausmaßen in der gesamten Provinz war. Es ist argentinisches Landleben de luxe – denn natürlich dürfen auf La Paz auch zwei Polofelder nicht fehlen, auf denen nationale Turniere ausgetragen werden, sowie ein anspruchsvoller 18-Loch-Golfplatz, dessen Rasen so gepflegt wirkt, als stutzte der Chef-Greenkeeper jeden einzelnen Grashalm persönlich mit der Nagelschere. Wer nach einer guten Runde dann noch das Glück hat, im Restaurant typische »Cocina Criolla« oder gar ein Barbecue zu erleben, kann den einstigen Hausherren verstehen: Zwei Monate Sommerferien auf La Paz sind wirklich das absolute Minimum.

Buchtipp: »Das Aleph« von Jorge Luis Borges

Être l'hôte du président

« Mon engagement politique ne m'a jamais détourné d'une routine devenue chère à mes yeux : passer au moins deux mois à La Paz tous les étés. » Ces lignes viennent de la plume de Julio Argentino Roca, président de l'Argentine de 1880 à 1886 et de 1898 à 1904, et membre du groupe politique intellectuel « Generación del 80 », qui misait sur l'immigration, la croissance économique et une classe moyenne forte. Ces messieurs ne discutaient pas seulement leurs réformes dans la capitale, à Buenos Aires, mais aussi à 110 kilomètres de là, à Ascochinga, dans la maison de campagne du président. Pour Julio Argentino Roca, La Paz était à la fois une résidence d'été et un lieu de rencontre pour politiciens. L'Estancia dégage aujourd'hui encore cette atmosphère. L'hôte réside dans des bâtiments peints en jaune et restaurés avec amour dans le style colonial et de la Renaissance italienne. Il peut flâner dans l'immense parc aménagé par le paysagiste français Charles Thays ou plonger dans la piscine qui, sur la demande de Roca, fut la première de toute l'Argentine à être de dimension olympique. La vie de campagne est luxueuse à La Paz : il n'y manque ni les deux terrains de polo, où se déroulent les compétitions nationales, ni le golf à 18 trous, dont chaque brin d'herbe semble avoir été coupé au ciseau à ongles par le greenkeeper en personne. Si après une partie, on a encore la chance de déguster la typique « cocina criolla » ou un barbecue au restaurant, on peut alors comprendre le maître de maison de jadis : deux mois d'été à La Paz sont le strict minimum.

Livre à emporter : « L'Aleph » de Jorge Luis Borges

ANREISE	50 Kilometer nordöstlich des Flughafens Córdoba gelegen (dorthin Inlandsflüge ab Buenos Aires)
PREIS	$$–$$$
ZIMMER	10 Zimmer
KÜCHE	Regionale Spezialitäten (Cocina Criolla) und typisch argentinisches Barbecue (Asado)
GESCHICHTE	Aus dem einstigen Landsitz des Präsidenten wurde ein luxuriöses Landhotel
X-FAKTOR	Sommerfrische auf staatsmännische Art

ACCÈS	Situé à 50 kilomètres au nord-est de l'aéroport de Córdoba (vols intérieurs depuis Buenos Aires)
PRIX	$$–$$$
CHAMBRES	10 chambres
RESTAURATION	Spécialités régionales (cocina criolla) et barbecue typiquement argentin (asado)
HISTOIRE	L'ancienne résidence du président a été transformée en hôtel luxueux
LES « PLUS »	Passer l'été comme un chef d'État

A literary trip...
Los Alamos, Mendoza

Los Alamos, Mendoza

A literary trip

"She is wherever there is music and the gentle blue of the sky" – thus wrote Argentina's most famous writer, Jorge Luis Borges, of his fellow writer Susana Bombal. Today you can see for yourself just how close the two were to each other – at Los Alamos, once the country residence of Bombal. About 1920 she became the owner of this venerable old family property in the midst of the Mendoza wine-growing district, and transformed it into a meeting place for the intelligentsia. It was a favourite place not only for Jorge Luis Borges but also for Silvina Ocampo (one of the leading women poets) and Manuel Mujica Láinez, who achieved fame as a journalist on the daily *La Nación* – both regularly spent weekends at Los Alamos. To this day the cosy rooms can be seen where this circle once gathered, and you can browse in the substantial library or see where Susana Bombal wrote the majority of her works, or admire paintings by Borges' sister Norah. The interior décor emphasizes a personal, country style, with terracotta hues, delicately painted tiles, and dark furniture. It has just five guest rooms – but they are opulent, and one even boasts a billiards table. When you are resident here, you will be spoilt with traditional Argentine fare, but you'll also have ample opportunity to work off any surplus calories. There are walks to be taken through the surrounding vineyards, there's trout fishing and duck shooting, and there's horse riding in the Andes. And if you're in for adventures on water, there's rafting in the nearby canyons. And finally, if relaxing with an evening's musical entertainment is your preference, Los Alamos offers Argentine barbecues followed by dancing.

Book to pack: "Selected Poems" by Jorge Luis Borges

Los Alamos
San Rafael
Mendoza
Argentina
Tel: + 54 (9260) 4405 955 and 4531 310
E-mail: bombalagro@infovia.com.ar
No website

DIRECTIONS	Situated 200 km/125 miles south of Mendoza airport (regular domestic flights from Buenos Aires)
RATES	$$$
ROOMS	5 double rooms
FOOD	Mouth-watering home cooking following old family recipes
HISTORY	Built in 1830, the property was formerly the country residence of writer Susana Bombal. It is still family owned
X-FACTOR	Life in the country, pure and simple – just as Argentina's novelists describe it

Eine literarische Reise

»Sie ist dort, wo Musik ist und das sanfte Blau des Himmels« – das schrieb Argentiniens berühmtester Autor Jorge Luis Borges über seine Kollegin Susana Bombal. Wie nahe sich die beiden standen, kann man heute noch nachvollziehen – in Los Alamos, dem einstigen Landsitz der Schriftstellerin. Mitten in der Weinregion Mendoza übernahm Susana Bombal um 1920 den altehrwürdigen Familienbesitz und verwandelte ihn in einen Treffpunkt der Intellektuellen. Hier fand nicht nur Jorge Luis Borges einen seiner Lieblingsplätze; auch Silvina Ocampo (»Gedichte einer verzweifelten Liebe«) und Manuel Mujica Láinez, der als Journalist der Tageszeitung »La Nación« berühmt wurde, verbrachten regelmäßig ihr Wochenende auf Los Alamos. Noch heute kann man die gemütlichen Räume besichtigen, in denen sich die Zirkel einst trafen, sich durch die gut sortierte Bibliothek lesen, einen Blick in das Zimmer werfen, in dem Susana Bombal die meisten ihrer Werke schrieb, oder Gemälde von Borges' Schwester Norah bewundern. Das Haus ist im persönlichen Countrystil ausgestattet, setzt auf Terrakottatöne, filigran bemalte Fliesen und dunkle Möbel und besitzt nur fünf opulente Gästezimmer (in einem prangt sogar ein Billardtisch). Wer hier wohnt, wird mit argentinischer Hausmannskost nach überlieferten Rezepten verwöhnt, hat aber reichlich Gelegenheit, die Kalorien wieder abzutrainieren. Zur Auswahl stehen Spaziergänge durch die umliegenden Weinberge, Forellenfischen und die Entenjagd oder Ausritte in die Anden. Wer Wasser nicht scheut, kann zudem durch die nahen Canyons raften; und für alle, die am liebsten bei Musik entspannen, bietet Los Alamos argentinische Grillabende mit anschließendem Tanz.

Buchtipp: »Der Geschmack eines Apfels« von Jorge Luis Borges

Un voyage littéraire

« Elle est là où sont la musique et le bleu du ciel », a écrit Jorge Luis Borges, l'auteur le plus célèbre d'Argentine, sur sa collègue Susana Bombal. Leur complicité mutuelle se constate aujourd'hui encore, à Los Alamos, l'ancienne résidence de la femme écrivain. En 1920, Susana Bombal reprit la propriété familiale située en pleine région viticole pour la transformer en lieu de rencontre des intellectuels. Ce fut l'endroit préféré de Jorge Luis Borges. Quant à Silvina Ocampo (« Poèmes d'amour désespéré ») et Manuel Mujica Láinez, célèbre journaliste du quotidien « La Nación », ils passaient tous leurs week-ends à Los Alamos. De nos jours, on peut encore visiter les pièces confortables où les membres du cercle se réunissaient, lire les ouvrages de la bibliothèque, jeter un regard dans le bureau où Susana Bombal a écrit la plupart de ses livres ou admirer les tableaux de Norah, la sœur de Borges. La maison est décorée dans un style country personnel, affectionne les tons de terre cuite, le carrelage finement peint et les meubles sombres, et elle possède cinq chambres d'hôtes généreuses où trône même dans l'une d'elles une table de billard. Celui qui réside ici aura le plaisir de trouver une gastronomie argentine préparée selon des recettes traditionnelles. Mais n'ayez crainte, vous aurez amplement l'occasion de brûler vos calories. La maison propose au choix des promenades dans les vignobles alentour, la pêche à la truite, la chasse au canard ou des randonnées à cheval dans les Andes. Ceux qui ne craignent pas l'eau pourront faire du rafting dans les proches canyons et pour tous ceux qui préfèrent se détendre avec de la musique, Los Alamos offre des soirées dansantes commençant par un barbecue argentin.

Livre à emporter : « L'art de poésie » de Jorge Luis Borges

ANREISE	200 Kilometer südlich des Flughafens Mendoza gelegen (dorthin regelmäßige Inlandsflüge ab Buenos Aires)
PREIS	$$$
ZIMMER	5 Doppelzimmer
KÜCHE	Traumhafte Hausmannskost nach alten Familienrezepten
GESCHICHTE	1830 erbaut und ehemaliger Landsitz der Schriftstellerin Susana Bombal. Noch heute in Familienbesitz
X-FAKTOR	Landleben pur – so schön wie in argentinischen Romanen

ACCÈS	Situé à 200 kilomètres au sud de l'aéroport de Mendoza (vols intérieurs réguliers depuis Buenos Aires)
PRIX	$$$
CHAMBRES	5 chambres doubles
CUISINE	Merveilleuse cuisine maison selon de vieilles recettes de famille
HISTOIRE	Construite en 1830, c'est l'ancienne résidence de l'écrivain Susana Bombal. Se trouve aujourd'hui encore en possession de la famille
LES « PLUS »	La vie à la campagne par excellence – aussi belle que dans les romans argentins

A natural beauty...
La Becasina Delta Lodge, Province Buenos Aires

La Becasina Delta Lodge, Province Buenos Aires

A natural beauty

Amazing to think town and country can be so close and yet so far apart: just a few miles out of Buenos Aires you come to the Paraná delta, an enchanting landscape of small waterways and lush vegetation, where life seems to move in slow motion, as if bedded on velvet. It's the perfect place to while away the days paddling a kayak on the river, watching the birds and listening to their shrill, wondrous calls, or fishing from the riverbank in a mood so peaceful that bristling appointments diaries and ceaselessly jangling mobiles seem a world away. In the heart of this idyllic realm, La Becasina Delta Lodge awaits its guests. It's situated on the bank of the Arroyo Las Cañas, with marshlands around it that have largely remained unspoilt. The few stray buildings supported on stilts seem almost to hover above the water, and are linked by wooden walkways or bridges. Every one of the 15 bungalow suites has all the charisma of a private residence – for a few happy days, you are the owner of a humble lodging of understated luxury, with a dream veranda and views of the greenery. If you don't only want to admire the water from a dry haven, why not take time out on the river in a boat, or indeed *in* it? The only imperative rule is always to swim against the current – otherwise you'll be borne away from paradise all too swiftly…

Book to pack: "Mascaro, the American Hunter" by Haroldo Conti

La Becasina Delta Lodge
Arroyo Las Cañas, San Fernando
C1021AAH, Buenos Aires
Argentina
Tel: + 54 (11) 4728 1395 and 4328 2687
E-mail: reservas@labecasina.com
Website: www.labecasina.com

DIRECTIONS	Situated some 60 km/38 miles north of Buenos Aires. One-hour boat transfer from San Fernando/Tigre US$ 30 per person
RATES	$$$
ROOMS	15 bungalow suites for 2 people
FOOD	Argentine specialities and wines
HISTORY	Opened in 2007
X-FACTOR	Everything is in flow – feel good by the water

Natürlich schön

So nahe können Stadt und Land nebeneinanderliegen und so fern können sich beide Welten sein: Man muss nur ein paar Kilometer aus Buenos Aires hinausfahren und schon erreicht man das Paraná-Delta, eine Märchenlandschaft mit kleinen Wasserwegen und üppiger Vegetation, in der das Leben noch in Zeitlupe und wie unter Samt gelegen abläuft. Hier kann man seine Tage damit verbringen, mit dem Kajak auf den Fluss hinauszupaddeln, den Vögeln hinterherzusehen und ihren schrill-schönen Rufen zu lauschen oder mit so viel See-lenruhe am Ufer zu angeln, als hätte man niemals Wochen voller berstender Terminkalender und im Sekundentakt klingelnder Handys erlebt. Inmitten dieses Idylls wartet die La Becasina Delta Lodge auf Gäste – am Ufer des Arroyo Las Cañas gelegen und um sich herum eine Sumpflandschaft, die ihren ursprünglichen Charakter noch weitgehend erhalten konnte. Die einzelnen Gebäude scheinen auf ihren Stelzen über dem Wasser zu schweben und sind über hölzerne Stege oder Brücken miteinander verbunden. Jede der 15 Bunga-lowsuiten besitzt das Flair einer Privatadresse – für ein paar glückliche Tage ist man Besitzer eines Häuschens mit dezen-tem Luxus und einer traumhaften Veranda mit Blick ins Grü-ne. Wer das Wasser nicht nur vom Trockenen aus bewundern will, kann an Bootsausflügen teilnehmen oder ganz einfach im Fluss untertauchen. Dabei gilt nur eine einzige Regel: Immer gegen die Strömung schwimmen – sonst wird man allzu schnell vom Paradies weggetrieben.

Buchtipp: »Op Oloop« von Juan Filloy

Des vacances au naturel

Buenos Aires, la capitale trépidante, ne se trouve qu'à quelques kilomètres, et pourtant elle semble très loin d'ici. En fait nous sommes dans un autre monde, celui du delta du Paraná, véritable paysage de conte de fées avec ses ca-naux et sa végétation luxuriante. Ici, la vie s'écoule encore au ralenti, comme si elle glissait sur du velours. On peut passer ses journées en kayak sur le fleuve à regarder les oiseaux et écouter leurs beaux cris perçants ou pêcher sur les rives en toute sérénité. Envolés les agendas bourrés de rendez-vous urgents, oubliée la sonnerie incessante des portables. Située sur la rive de l'Arroyo Las Cañas, entourée d'un paysage de marécages qui a su préserver son caractère original, La Beca-sina Delta Lodge attend ses hôtes pour partager avec eux ce site idyllique. Les constructions sur pilotis, reliées entre elles par des passerelles en bois et des pontons, semblent flotter au-dessus de l'eau. Chaque suite-bungalow a son caractère particulier – pendant quelques jours, on sera l'heureux pro-priétaire d'une maisonnette au luxe sobre dotée d'une véran-da de rêve s'ouvrant sur la verdure. Et ceux qui ne veulent pas se contenter d'admirer l'eau de loin peuvent participer à des sorties en bateau ou tout simplement se baigner, en veillant cependant à nager contre le courant – sinon ils seraient trop vite entraînés loin de ce paradis.

Livre à emporter : « La ballade du peuplier carolin » de Haroldo Conti

ANREISE	Rund 60 Kilometer nördlich von Buenos Aires gele-gen. Einstündiger Bootstransfer ab San Fernando/Tigre US$ 30 pro Person
PREIS	$$$
ZIMMER	15 Bungalowsuiten für je 2 Personen
KÜCHE	Argentinische Spezialitäten und Weine
GESCHICHTE	2007 eröffnet
X-FAKTOR	Alles fließt – Wohlfühlen am Wasser

ACCÈS	Situé à 60 kilomètres au nord de Buenos Aires. À une heure de bateau de San Fernando/Tigre, US$ 30 par personne
PRIX	$$$
CHAMBRES	15 suites-bungalows pour 2 personnes
RESTAURATION	Spécialités et vins argentins
HISTOIRE	Ouvert depuis 2007
LES « PLUS »	Au fil de l'eau

Rooms with a family connecti

Estancia El Rosario de Areco, Province Buenos Aires

Estancia El Rosario de Areco,
Province Buenos Aires

Rooms with a family connection

For Juan Francisco Guevara and his wife Florencia, family is the main thing in life. The owners of El Rosario de Areco have nine children and four grandchildren – and like to have them around as much as possible. So their estancia truly is a family business. The six sons in particular do sterling work at this hotel 115 kilometres (75 miles) from Buenos Aires, seeing to guests from all over the world who've come to enjoy the Argentine countryside. This being horse-crazy Argentina, there are special pleasures to indulge in too: El Rosario de Areco is a famed polo club with two pitches of its own and even its own team, which turns out to regional and national tournaments. If you feel like a go at smashing the ball across the grass without falling out of the saddle yourself, you can take private tuition from professional jockeys here or even book a whole week's polo. For everyone else, the estancia does arrange horse riding of the usual kind, or you can take walks around the estate or head for a dip in the pool. The house itself is in a modern, plain country style, with walls in warm natural hues, soft inviting sofas by the fireside, and sturdy stoneware all contributing to that authentic country house feel. The genuine home cooking is in tune with the atmosphere – from fresh milk at breakfast to plaited loaves warm from the oven in the afternoon to grilled beef in the evening. This is an estancia not just for private vacationers: El Rosario de Areco also offers events and incentives for companies: car manufacturers, universities, and banks from around the world have already used the facilities.

Book to pack: "A Change of Light and Other Stories" by Julio Cortázar

Estancia El Rosario de Areco
Casilla de Correo 85
2760 San Antonio de Areco
Argentina
Tel: + 54 (2325) 650 690
E-mail: estancia@rosariodeareco.com.ar
Website: www.rosariodeareco.com.ar

DIRECTIONS	Situated 115 km/75 miles northwest of Buenos Aires
RATES	$$$
ROOMS	14 suites, 1 senior suite
FOOD	Hearty home cooking
HISTORY	A country residence built in 1892, converted into a hotel
X-FACTOR	A riding holiday for all the family – with a whole family

Zimmer mit Familienanschluss

Für Juan Francisco Guevara und seine Frau Florencia ist die Familie das Wichtigste. Neun Kinder und vier Enkel haben die Besitzer von El Rosario de Areco – und alle am liebsten so oft wie möglich um sich herum. Deshalb ist ihre Estancia auch ein echter Familienbetrieb. Vor allem die sechs Söhne kümmern sich im Hotel um die Gäste aus aller Welt, die hier, 115 Kilometer von Buenos Aires entfernt, argentinische Landluft schnuppern wollen. Durch diese weht im pferdeverrückten Argentinien vor allem Stallduft: El Rosario de Areco besitzt als renommierter Poloklub zwei eigene Spielfelder und sogar eine eigene Mannschaft, die bei regionalen und nationalen Turnieren antritt. Wer es den Männern nachmachen und den Ball, möglichst ohne aus dem Sattel zu fallen, über den Rasen schlagen will, kann hier Privatstunden bei professionellen Jockeys nehmen oder gleich eine ganze Polowoche buchen. Für alle anderen organisiert die Estancia aber auch ganz normale Ausritte oder Spaziergänge durch den umliegenden Park und lässt sie anschließend im Pool untertauchen. Das Haus selbst bietet modernen und schlichten Countrystil; in warmen Naturtönen getünchte Wände, kuschelige Sofas am Kamin und robustes Steingut sorgen für unverfälschtes Landhausflair. Passend dazu setzt die Küche auf echte Hausmannskost – inklusive frischer Milch zum Frühstück, ofenwarmen Hefezöpfen am Nachmittag und gegrilltem Rind am Abend. Auf den Geschmack sind übrigens nicht nur Privaturlauber gekommen: El Rosario de Areco veranstaltet auch Events oder Incentives für Firmen; zu Gast waren bereits internationale Autohäuser, Universitäten und Banken.

Buchtipp: »Passatwinde« von Julio Cortázar

Être accueilli dans une famille

Pour Juan Francisco Guevara et sa femme Frau Florencia la famille est la chose la plus importante. Il faut dire aussi que les propriétaires d'El Rosario de Areco ont neuf enfants et quatre petits-enfants et ce qu'ils préfèrent, c'est les avoir auprès d'eux le plus souvent possible. Leur Estancia est donc une véritable exploitation familiale. Les fils surtout s'occupent des clients du monde entier qui, à cent quinze kilomètres de Buenos Aires, désirent respirer un peu de la campagne argentine. Mais c'est aussi l'air des écuries que l'on sent dans cette Argentine éperdument éprise de chevaux : en tant que club de polo de grande renommée, El Rosario de Areco possède deux terrains et même une équipe qui dispute des tournois régionaux et internationaux. Celui qui veut imiter les joueurs et courir après la balle sans tomber de cheval peut prendre des cours particuliers auprès de jockeys professionnels ou réserver directement toute une semaine de polo. Pour tous les autres l'Estancia organise aussi des promenades à pied ou à cheval dans le parc, et propose sa piscine pour se détendre. La maison est décorée dans un style campagnard sobre et moderne. Les murs badigeonnés dans des tons chauds et naturels, les canapés moelleux près de la cheminée, les objets en grès dégagent une atmosphère authentique de maison de campagne. En accord avec cela, la cuisine mise sur les plats rustiques, y compris le lait qui vient d'être trait au petit déjeuner, les pains briochés sortis tout droit du four l'après-midi et les grillades de bœuf le soir. Les touristes ne sont pas les seuls à goûter toutes ces joies : El Rosario de Areco organise aussi des journées spéciales pour les sociétés. Des concessionnaires automobiles, des universités et des banques du monde entier ont déjà été leurs hôtes.

Livre à emporter : « Le fantastique argentin » de Julio Cortázar

ANREISE	115 Kilometer nordwestlich von Buenos Aires gelegen
PREIS	$$$
ZIMMER	14 Suiten, 1 Senior Suite
KÜCHE	Herzhaft und hausgemacht
GESCHICHTE	Ein 1892 errichteter Landsitz wurde zum Hotel umgebaut
X-FAKTOR	Reiterferien für die ganze Familie – bei einer ganzen Familie

ACCÈS	Situé à 115 kilomètres au nord-ouest de Buenos Aires
PRIX	$$$
CHAMBRES	14 suites, 1 Senior Suite
RESTAURATION	Cuisine maison savoureuse
HISTOIRE	Maison de campagne construite en 1892, puis transformée en hôtel
LES « PLUS »	Vacances équestres pour toute la famille et chez une famille

King for a day...

Estancia La Candelaria, Province Buenos Aires

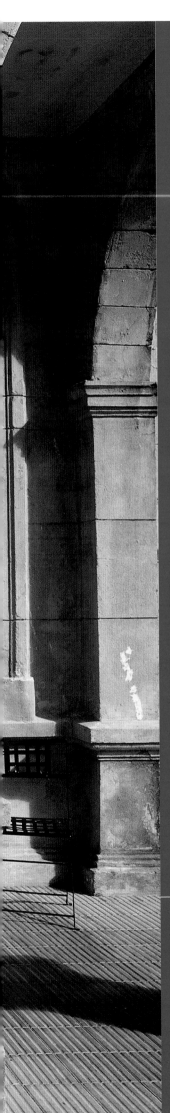

Estancia La Candelaria,
Province Buenos Aires

King for a day

At first glance you'd think this castle with its turrets, battlements, and high windows belonged in the Loire Valley, or maybe Eurodisney near Paris – if it weren't for the fact that it's in this breathtaking tropical garden. More than 240 different trees and plants grow here, such as palms, eucalyptus trees, or banana plants. A gleaming white bridge spans a modest watercourse, and the grass shines as if it had been sprayed with bright green paint. The park was created by the famous landscape architect Charles Thays, and the château fits into it perfectly. The residence was built in the mid-19th century by pharmacist and sheep breeder Don Orestes Piñeiro, who named it after his wife, Doña Candelaria Del Marmol. La Candelaria was the family's other world, their retreat in the solitude of the Argentine pampas, far from civilisation. And although the region is now perfectly accessible, and anything but backwoods, the château remains a quiet refuge to get away to. You reside in spacious rooms beneath coffered ceilings and crystal chandeliers. The floors are gleaming parquet or costly carpet, the armchairs are carved, and the beds have gilded bedsteads. La Candelaria is a return to a magnificent era long thought forgotten, and guests here can be king for a while. The pastimes all strike the right note of class, among them billiards, tennis, golf, and polo. The property still belongs to the same family, and while the owners may be deeply attached to the past, they also have a real sense of the present: all the sporting and leisure activities are included in the room price. This is Argentina all inclusive.

Book to pack: "Voices" by Antonio Porchia

Estancia La Candelaria	
Ruta 205, km 114.5	
Lobos, Buenos Aires	
Argentina	
Tel: + 54 (2227) 494 132 and 494 473	
Fax: + 54 (2227) 494 132	
E-mail: info@estanciacandelaria.com	
Website: www.estanciacandelaria.com	

DIRECTIONS	Situated 115 km/75 miles northeast of Buenos Aires.
RATES	$$$$
ROOMS	2 double rooms in bungalows, 1 double in the old mill, 10 double in colonial houses, 10 double and suites in the château
FOOD	Refined Argentine and international cuisine
HISTORY	A picture-book retreat, family-owned since 1840
X-FACTOR	My palace, my park, my polo pitch

Heute ein König

Auf den ersten Blick würde man dieses Schloss mit seinen spitzen Türmen, Zinnen und hohen Fenstern eher im Tal der Loire oder im Disneyland bei Paris vermuten – stünde es nicht in diesem traumhaften tropischen Garten. Hier gedeihen mehr als 240 verschiedene Pflanzen wie Palmen, Eukalyptusbäume oder Bananenstauden, über einen kleinen Wasserlauf spannt sich eine strahlend weiße Brücke, und der Rasen leuchtet, als habe man ihn mit hellgrüner Farbe besprüht. Der Park trägt die Handschrift des berühmten Landschaftsarchitekten Charles Thays, und das Château passt dazu wie das Tüpfelchen auf dem i. Mitte des 19. Jahrhunderts ließ der Apotheker und Schafzüchter Don Orestes Piñeiro das Anwesen bauen und benannte es nach seiner Frau, Doña Candelaria Del Marmol. Mit La Candelaria schuf sich die Familie eine andere Welt – in der Einsamkeit der argentinischen Pampa und fern jeglicher Zivilisation gelegen. Und obwohl die Region inzwischen gut erschlossen und alles andere als hinterwäldlerisch ist, ist diese Adresse noch immer ein Fluchtpunkt und ein ruhiges Refugium. Hier residiert man in weiten Räumen unter Kassettendecken oder Kristalllüstern, schreitet über glänzendes Parkett oder wertvolle Teppiche, thront auf geschnitzten Lehnstühlen oder in goldumrahmten Betten. La Candelaria lässt eine prachtvolle und längst vergessen geglaubte Epoche wieder aufleben und verwandelt seine Gäste in Schlossherren auf Zeit. Zum standesgemäßen Vergnügen gehören auch Billard, Tennis, Golf und Polo – und dass die Besitzer (das Areal ist immer noch in Familienbesitz) trotz aller Liebe zur Vergangenheit längst in der Gegenwart angekommen sind, zeigt sich daran, dass alle Sport- und Freizeitaktivitäten im Zimmerpreis eingeschlossen sind: Das ist Argentinien *all inclusive*.
Buchtipp: »Verlassene Stimmen« von Antonio Porchia

Se sentir comme un roi

On pourrait croire au premier abord que ce château avec ses tours, ses créneaux et ses hautes fenêtres se trouve dans la Vallée de la Loire ou à Dysneyland près de Paris, s'il n'était pas entouré de ces merveilleux jardins tropicaux, dans lesquels poussent plus de 240 espèces différentes de plantes, comme des palmiers, des eucalyptus et des bananiers. Un pont d'un blanc éclatant passe au-dessus d'un petit cours d'eau et la pelouse resplendit comme si on l'avait peinte de couleur verte. Le parc porte la signature du célèbre paysagiste Charles Thays et s'accorde parfaitement avec le château. C'est au milieu du XIXᵉ siècle que l'apothicaire et éleveur de moutons Don Orestes Piñeiro fit construire sa demeure et la baptisa d'après sa femme, Doña Candelaria Del Marmol. Avec La Candelaria la famille s'est créé un autre univers, dans la solitude de la pampa argentine et loin de toute civilisation. Et même si la région est maintenant bien développée et tout sauf sauvage, cette adresse demeure encore un refuge tranquille. Ici, on réside dans de larges pièces sous un plafond à cassettes et des lustres en cristal, on marche sur un parquet reluisant ou des tapis précieux, on trône sur des fauteuils en bois sculpté ou on se prélasse dans des lits dorés. La Candelaria fait revivre une époque somptueuse que l'on croyait depuis longtemps révolue et transforme pour un temps ses hôtes en châtelains. Pour se divertir dignement, on aura le choix entre le billard, le tennis, le golf et le polo. Malgré leur amour pour le passé, les propriétaires (la résidence est encore entre les mains de la famille) ont les deux pieds dans le présent et cela se voit dans le fait que toutes les activités sportives ou non sont comprises dans le prix de la chambre : c'est l'Argentine *all inclusive*.
Livre à emporter : « Voix abandonnées » d'Antonio Porchia

ANREISE	115 Kilometer nordöstlich von Buenos Aires gelegen
PREIS	$$$$
ZIMMER	2 Doppelzimmer in Bungalows, 1 Doppelzimmer in der alten Mühle, 10 Doppelzimmer in traditionellen Kolonialhäusern, 10 Doppelzimmer und Suiten im Schloss
KÜCHE	Verfeinerte argentinische und internationale Küche
GESCHICHTE	Familienbesitz wie aus dem Bilderbuch – seit 1840
X-FAKTOR	Mein Palast, mein Park, mein Polofeld

ACCÈS	Situé à 115 kilomètres de Buenos Aires
PRIX	$$$$
CHAMBRES	2 chambres doubles en bungalow, 1 chambre double dans l'ancien moulin, 10 chambres doubles dans les maisons coloniales traditionnelles, 10 chambres doubles et suites au château
RESTAURATION	Cuisine argentine et internationale de qualité
HISTOIRE	Entre les mains de la famille depuis 1840
LES « PLUS »	Mon palais, mon parc, mon terrain de polo

Living like in olden times...
Hotel del Casco, Province Buenos Aires

Hotel del Casco,
Province Buenos Aires

Living like in olden times

This journey back into the past takes you a mere 24 kilometres (15 miles) from Buenos Aires. It leads to San Isidro with its delightful historic centre – and the Hotel del Casco. This former town house in the neo-classical style of the 19th century is on Avenida del Libertador and looks so absolutely spick and span you'd think they dusted it top to bottom daily and polished every knob till it shone. With its flight of marble steps, high windows, and slender pillars it looks almost like a museum, keeping the charm of times past sequestered from view. The quiet of the coolly-tiled glass-roofed lobby, where ferns strike a note of colour under the arches, prompts new arrivals to speak in undertones – but it's a deference that's hardly necessary. Life is there to be enjoyed at the Hotel del Casco, be it in the garden, on the planted patio (the roof of which can be opened in fine weather), or in the rooms, their walls painted a Bordeaux red or lime green or covered in subtly patterned papers. Antiques of precious wood, crystal chandeliers, and free-standing bathtubs with claw feet create a classically stylish atmosphere – knick-knacks of the sort beloved by so many Argentine hotel proprietors will be sought here largely in vain. The note of aristocratic grace is upheld in the vicinity. Opposite the hotel is the Cathedral of San Isidro, the tower rising majestically into the heavens, and there are walks to be taken in tranquil gardens and parks or along the riverbank. And should this idyllic world ever seem too peaceful, it's the easiest thing to get back to the future: Buenos Aires is just 24 kilometres (15 miles) away.

Book to pack: "Artificial Respiration" by Ricardo Piglia

Hotel del Casco	
Avenida del Libertador 16.170 San Isidro	
B1642CVV Buenos Aires	
Argentina	
Tel: + 54 (11) 4732 3993	
Fax: + 54 (11) 4732 3993	
E-mail: info@hoteldelcasco.com.ar	
Website: www.hoteldelcasco.com.ar	

DIRECTIONS	Situated 24 km/15 miles northeast of Buenos Aires, 45 km /28 miles from the international airport (50 minutes by road)
RATES	$$
ROOMS	20 rooms, 2 apartments, 2 suites and 8 garden suites
FOOD	Classic Argentine cuisine
HISTORY	Located in a restored town residence built in 1892
X-FACTOR	Highly sophisticated

Wohnen wie in alten Zeiten

Die Reise von Buenos Aires zurück in die Vergangenheit ist nur 24 Kilometer lang. Sie führt nach San Isidro mit seinem hübschen historischen Zentrum – und mit dem Hotel del Casco. Die ehemalige Stadtresidenz im neoklassizistischen Stil des 19. Jahrhunderts steht an der Avenida del Libertador und sieht so rein und proper aus, als staubte man sie jeden Tag ab und polierte sie auf Hochglanz. Mit ihrer marmornen Freitreppe, den hohen Fenstern und schlanken Säulen wirkt sie fast wie ein Museum, das den Charme vergangener Zeiten birgt. Die Ruhe in der kühl gefliesten Lobby, in der Farne grüne Akzente setzen und über deren Bögen sich ein gläsernes Dach wölbt, lässt Neuankömmlinge unbewusst die Stimme senken – doch so viel Zurückhaltung ist gar nicht nötig. Im Hotel del Casco weiß man das Leben durchaus zu genießen, sei es im Garten, im bepflanzten Patio, dessen Dach bei schönem Wetter geöffnet werden kann, oder in den Zimmern, deren Wände in Bordeauxrot oder Lindgrün leuchten oder dezent gemusterte Tapeten besitzen. Antiquitäten aus wertvollem Holz, Kristallleuchter und frei stehende Badewannen mit geschwungenen Füßen sorgen für klassisch-elegantes Ambiente – Krimskrams und Nippes, den viele argentinische Hoteliers sonst so lieben, sucht man hier fast vergebens. Auf aristokratischen Pfaden wandeln kann man auch in der unmittelbaren Nachbarschaft: Gleich gegenüber dem Hotel steht die Kathedrale von San Isidro, deren Turm majestätisch in den Himmel ragt, und man spaziert durch ruhige Gärten und Parks oder am Flussufer entlang. Und sollte einem das Idyll doch einmal zu ruhig erscheinen, kommt man im Handumdrehen zurück in die Zukunft: Buenos Aires ist ja nur 24 Kilometer entfernt.

Buchtipp: »Künstliche Atmung« von Ricardo Piglia

Un voyage dans le passé

Pour voyager dans le passé, il suffit de se rendre à 24 kilomètres de Buenos Aires, dans le joli centre historique de San Isidro, et de résider à l'hôtel del Casco. L'ancien palais construit dans le style néo-classique du XIXᵉ siècle se trouve sur l'Avenida del Libertador et a l'air si resplendissant qu'on a l'impression qu'on lui enlève tous les jours sa poussière et qu'on le fait ensuite reluire avec un chiffon. Avec son escalier en marbre, ses hautes fenêtres et ses minces colonnes il ressemble presque à un musée qui abriterait tout le charme des époques passées. Le calme qui règne à la réception, recouverte d'un toit en verre et où les fougères ajoutent une petite note de vert, est si impressionnant que les nouveaux venus baissent directement le ton – mais une telle réserve n'est pas nécessaire. À l'hôtel del Casco on sait profiter de la vie, que ce soit dans le jardin, dans le patio verdoyant dont le toit peut être ouvert les jours de beau temps, ou dans les chambres aux murs rouge bordeaux et vert tilleul et dont le sol est recouvert de tapis aux motifs décents. Les antiquités en bois précieux, les lustres en cristal et les baignoires aux pieds recourbés procurent une ambiance classique et élégante, et l'on cherchera en vain toutes ces babioles que les hôteliers argentins aiment tant. Dehors on restera dans cette même ambiance puisqu'en face de l'hôtel se trouve la cathédrale de San Isidro, dont la tour s'élève majestueusement dans le ciel, et l'on se promènera dans les parcs et jardins tranquilles ou le long de la rivière. Et si cette atmosphère idyllique nous semble un peu trop calme, on se retrouvera en un rien de temps à notre époque moderne, car Buenos Aires n'est qu'à 24 kilomètres de là.

Livre à emporter : « Respiration artificielle » de Ricardo Piglia

ANREISE	24 Kilometer nordöstlich von Buenos Aires gelegen, 45 Kilometer vom Internationalen Flughafen entfernt (50 Minuten Fahrtzeit)	ACCÈS	Situé à 24 kilomètres au nord-est de Buenos Aires, à 45 kilomètres de l'aéroport (50 min. en voiture)
PREIS	$$	PRIX	$$
ZIMMER	20 Zimmer, 2 Apartments, 2 Suiten und 8 Gartensuiten	CHAMBRES	20 chambres, 2 appartements, 2 suites et 8 suites jardin
KÜCHE	Klassische argentinische Küche	RESTAURATION	Cuisine argentine classique
GESCHICHTE	In einem restaurierten Stadtpalais aus dem Jahr 1892 untergebracht	HISTOIRE	Palais restauré en 1892
X-FAKTOR	Sehr sophisticated	LES « PLUS »	Très sophistiqué

So far. So good...
Tipiliuke, Patagonia

Tipiliuke, Patagonia

So far. So good

Some hotels are so wonderful that you don't ever want to walk out of the door. In the case of the Tipiliuke (pronounced "Tip-i-lu-kay") things are a little different: if you don't go out, you miss everything, as the hotel is situated in something like a "best of Patagonia". Two crystal-clear rivers flow through the huge country estate to which the lodge belongs. Moreover, there is a unique fauna and flora right on the doorstep – the kinds of trees alone that you can explore add up to 200 different species. For spectacular fly fishing within sight of snow-covered peaks, horse riding in groups at sunset around the Lanín volcano or simply harvesting vegetables in the hotel's own organic garden – getting fresh air in the finest possible way is part of the programme here every day. Despite the unbeatable outdoors, the warm-heartedness of the hosts is the first thing mentioned by most guests who have found their way to this austere paradise. The owners manage to involve their guests in a perfectly straightforward way in the everyday life of the gauchos on the ranch and quickly convey to every visitor a family feeling, a sense of being well cared-for. This includes cosy gatherings by the fireplace and an open bar where one and all can help themselves, but also luxurious amenities and discreetly efficient service. Elegant British country-house style and the aura of gentleman's sports that can be pursued here make a stay at the Tipiliuke an adventure with a guarantee of wellbeing. And then, of course, you never want to leave the place again.

Book to pack: "In Patagonia" by Bruce Chatwin

Tipiliuke
San Martín de los Andes
Patagonia
Argentina
Tel: + 54 (2972) 429 466 (lodge)
Tel: + 54 (911) 4199 2228 (reservations)
Closed in June
E-mail: info@tipiliuke.com
Website: www.tipiliuke.com

DIRECTIONS	Two hours' flight southwest of Buenos Aires; transfer to the lodge is included and only takes ten minutes
RATES	$$$$
ROOMS	9 modern, rustic-style rooms in the lodge, 2 houses with 5 rooms (can only be booked together)
FOOD	Outstanding refined traditional dishes and Argentinian wines
HISTORY	The ranch was founded in 1909 by ancestors of the current owner. Since the 1990s it has accommodated keen fly fishers
X-FACTOR	The ranch is still in operation; the house is therefore ideal for guests who would like to be cowboys for a while

So weit, so gut

Es gibt Hotels, die sind so schön, dass man sie gar nicht mehr verlassen möchte. Im Falle des Tipiliuke (ausgesprochen „Tip-i-lu-kee") liegt die Sache etwas anders: Wer hier nicht rausgeht, verpasst alles, denn vor der Tür liegt eine Art *Best of Patagonia*. Zwei kristallklare Flüsse durchqueren den riesigen Landsitz, zu dem die Lodge gehört, und dazu befindet sich eine einzigartige Fauna und Flora direkt vor der Tür – allein 200 verschiedene Baumarten gibt es zu entdecken. Ob spektakuläres Fliegenfischen im Angesicht schneebedeckter Gipfel, Gruppenausritte zum Sonnenuntergang am Lanín-Vulkan oder auch nur Gemüseernten im hoteleigenen Biogarten – Frischluftakquise in ihrer schönsten Form steht hier jeden Tag auf dem Stundenplan. Trotz dieser unschlagbaren äußeren Werte erzählen die meisten Gäste, die sich in dieses herbe Paradies aufgemacht haben, als Erstes von der Herzlichkeit der Gastgeber. Sie schaffen es, ihre Gäste ganz unkompliziert in den Alltag der Gauchos auf der Ranch einzubinden und vermitteln an diesem Ort jedem Besucher schnell ein familiäres Gefühl der Geborgenheit. Dazu gehören gemütliche Runden vor dem Kamin genauso wie die offene Bar, bei der sich jeder bedienen kann, aber auch luxuriöse Annehmlichkeiten und ein lautloser Service. Der elegante britische Landhaus-Style und die Aura der Gentlemen-Sportarten, denen man hier nachgehen kann, machen den Aufenthalt zum Abenteuer mit Wohlfühlgarantie. Und verlassen möchte man diesen Ort dann natürlich auch nicht mehr.

Buchtipp: »In Patagonien« von Bruce Chatwin

Merveilles du bout du monde

Certains hôtels sont si beaux qu'on ne peut se résoudre à en sortir. Au Tipiliuke (prononcez « Tip-i-lou-ké »), les choses sont un peu différentes : le visiteur qui ne met pas le pied dehors passe à côté d'une sorte de « best of » de la Patagonie. En effet, le lodge est situé sur un domaine traversé par deux rivières aux eaux cristallines et abritant une faune et une flore spectaculaires (avec ne serait-ce que 200 espèces d'arbres différentes à découvrir). Chaque jour, on y fait le plein d'air pur en pratiquant les activités les plus idylliques qui soient : pêche à la mouche avec les sommets enneigés pour toile de fond, sorties en groupe à cheval pour admirer le coucher de soleil sur le volcan Lanín ou un loisir tout simple comme récolter les légumes du potager bio de l'hôtel. Malgré ces atouts du cadre extérieur, la plupart des visiteurs qui ont trouvé le chemin de ce paradis sauvage évoquent en premier l'accueil chaleureux. Les hôteliers partagent en toute simplicité avec eux le quotidien des gauchos sur l'estancia et font en sorte que chacun se sent vite chez soi. Cela tient aux agréables moments passés au coin du feu et au bar où chacun est libre de se servir, mais aussi au confort luxueux et au service très discret. L'élégance du style campagnard britannique et l'aura qui enveloppe les sports de gentlemans que l'on peut pratiquer ici font d'un séjour au Tipiliuke une aventure placée sous le signe du bien-être. Et l'on n'a bien sûr aucune envie de quitter ces lieux.

Livre à emporter : « En Patagonie » de Bruce Chatwin

ANREISE	Zwei Flugstunden südwestlich von Buenos Aires; 10-minütiger Transfer zur Lodge ist inklusive
PREIS	$$$$
ZIMMER	9 modern-rustikale Zimmer in der Lodge, 2 Häuser mit 5 Zimmern (nur als Einheit zu mieten)
KÜCHE	Hervorragend verfeinerte traditionelle Gerichte und argentinische Weine
GESCHICHTE	Die Ranch wurde von den Vorfahren der heutigen Besitzer 1909 gegründet. Seit den 1990er-Jahren werden hier enthusiastische Fliegenfischer beherbergt
X-FAKTOR	Die Ranch ist noch in Betrieb; das Haus ist also ideal für jeden, der gern mal Cowboy sein möchte

ACCÈS	À deux heures d'avion au sud-ouest de Buenos Aires ; le transfert en voiture qui dure 10 minutes jusqu'au lodge est compris dans le prix
PRIX	$$$$
CHAMBRES	9 chambres en style rustique moderne dans le lodge, 2 maisons avec 5 chambres (à louer en entier)
RESTAURATION	Plats traditionnels revisités et vins argentins
HISTOIRE	Le ranch a été créé en 1909 par les ancêtres des propriétaires actuels. Depuis les années 1990, l'hôtel accueille les passionnés de pêche à la mouche
LES « PLUS »	L'estancia étant encore en activité, cet établissement est fait pour ceux qui ont envie de jouer au cow-boy

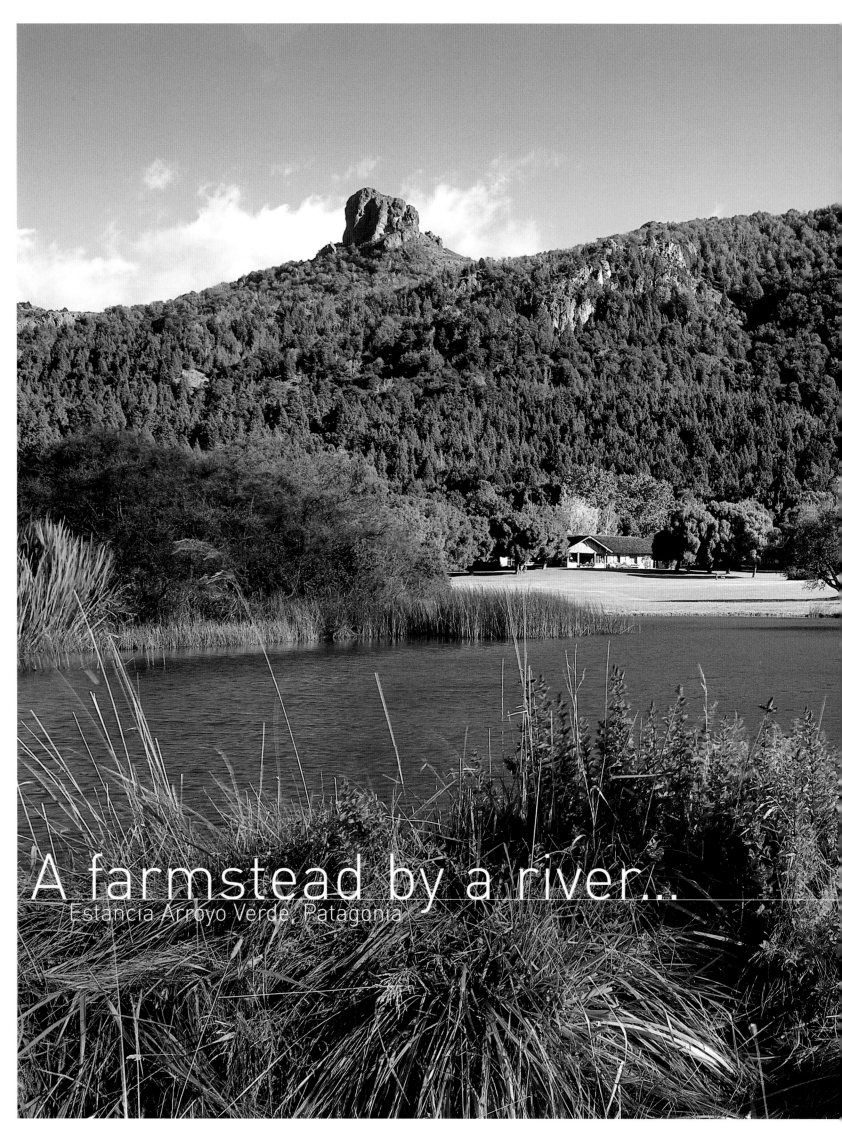

A farmstead by a river...
Estancia Arroyo Verde, Patagonia

Estancia Arroyo Verde, Patagonia

A farmstead by a river

The sparkling blue waters are crystal clear, and as it flows majestically through the valley it is brimful of salmon and trout – the Traful is every fly-fisher's dream. In the Nahuel Huapi National Park in northern Patagonia, where millions of years ago the earth was invisible beneath vast glaciers, the season opens on the second Saturday in November and runs till the third Sunday in April. Throughout those months the anglers are to be seen in their waders standing in the river, making their skilful (or in some cases not so skilful) casts and waiting patiently for the next bite. Most days the fish will weigh in at three to four pounds, and on a good day a ten-pounder will be reeled in from the Traful. If you like spending your time in the right kind of setting, among others who share your interests, book in to the Estancia Arroyo Verde and get a taste of Argentine country living at its best. Cattle and sheep graze the pastures at the foot of an impressive massif, and the stone and timber farmhouse itself is furnished in the South American country manner with deep armchairs, hunting trophies and knick-knacks. In the evenings, eat with silver cutlery off antique china, or barbecue down by the river if the weather's warm. For those who aren't here for the fishing alone, Arroyo Verde also offers riding and trekking in the Andes, or birdwatching in the land of the condor.

Book to pack: "Around the day in 80 worlds" by Julio Cortázar

Estancia Arroyo Verde
c/o Meme Larivière
Billinghurst 2586, 3° Piso
Buenos Aires
Argentina
Tel: + 54 (11) 4801 7448
E-mail: info@estanciaarroyoverde.com.ar
Website: www.estanciaarroyoverde.com.ar

DIRECTIONS	Situated 85 km/53 miles northwest of Bariloche airport
RATES	$$$–$$$$
ROOMS	6 double rooms in the main building, 1 lakeside chalet for 2 to 4
FOOD	International and Argentinian home cooking
HISTORY	A ranch was transformed into an adventure playground for those seeking an active holiday
X-FACTOR	One of South America's prime locations for fly-fishing

Die Farm am Fluss

Sein blau glitzerndes Wasser ist kristallklar, er fließt majestätisch durchs Tal und bringt ganze Schwärme von Lachsen und Forellen mit sich – der Traful ist der Traum aller Fliegenfischer. Im Norden Patagoniens, wo vor Millionen von Jahren riesige Gletscher die Erde bedeckten und sich heute der Nationalpark Nahuel Huapi ausdehnt, beginnt die Saison am zweiten Samstag im November und dauert bis zum dritten Sonntag im April. Dann stehen die Angler in hohen Gummistiefeln im Wasser, werfen mit (mehr oder weniger) wohlgeübten Bewegungen ihre langen Leinen aus und warten geduldig auf den nächsten Fang – drei bis vier Pfund bringen die Fische an normalen Tagen auf die Waage, an Glückstagen kann man aber durchaus auch einen satten Zehnpfünder aus den Fluten ziehen. Wer standesgemäß und unter Gleichgesinnten wohnen möchte, reserviert am besten in der Estancia Arroyo Verde und erlebt dort das argentinische Landleben *at its best*. Auf den Weiden am Fuß eines beeindruckenden Felsmassivs werden Rinder und Schafe gezüchtet, das Farmhaus aus Stein und Holz ist im südamerikanischen Countrystil mit viel Nippes, Jagdtrophäen sowie tiefen Sesseln zum Versinken eingerichtet, und man isst abends mit Silberbesteck von antikem Porzellan oder grillt bei warmem Wetter am Flussufer. Für alle, die ihre Tage nicht nur mit den Fischen verbringen wollen, bietet Arroyo Verde auch Ausritte und Trekkingtouren in den Anden an oder schickt sie zum Birdwatching auf den Spuren des Condors.

Buchtipp: »Reise um den Tag in 80 Welten« von Julio Cortázar

Le ranch au bord du fleuve

Il coule majestueusement à travers la vallée, ses eaux sont d'une pureté cristalline et elles regorgent de saumons et de truites. Le Traful est bien le paradis des pêcheurs. Dans le nord de la Patagonie, là où s'étendaient d'énormes glaciers il y a plusieurs millions d'années et où se trouve aujourd'hui le parc national de Nahuel Huapi, la saison de la pêche au lancer commence le deuxième samedi du mois de novembre pour se terminer le troisième dimanche du mois d'avril. Pendant cette période, les pêcheurs qui ont enfilé leurs cuissardes lancent leur ligne avec plus ou moins d'adresse et attendent patiemment que le poisson morde. En général, les poissons qu'ils attrapent pèsent entre trois et quatre livres, ce qui n'est pas négligeable, mais les jours de chance ils peuvent aussi avoir une belle prise qui pèsera ses dix livres sur la balance. Celui qui désire résider dans un hôtel de qualité parmi des gens qui partagent ses goûts, sera bien avisé de réserver une chambre à l'Estancia Arroyo Verde où il pourra aussi découvrir la vie à la campagne sous son meilleur côté. Des élevages de bœufs et de moutons paissent tranquillement dans les prairies au pied d'une formation rocheuse impressionnante. Le ranch, construit en pierre et en bois, présente un style campagnard sud-américain, avec beaucoup de bibelots, de trophées de chasse et de fauteuils dont la mollesse et la profondeur invitent au repos. Le soir, on sort l'argenterie et la porcelaine ou, quand le temps s'y prête, on organise un barbecue sur la rive du fleuve. Pour ceux qui ne désirent pas s'adonner à la pêche toute la journée, Arroyo Verde propose aussi des randonnées à pied ou à cheval dans les Andes ainsi que la possibilité de partir sur les traces du condor.

Livre à emporter : « Le tour du jour en 80 mondes » de Julio Cortázar

ANREISE	85 Kilometer nordwestlich des Flughafens Bariloche
PREIS	$$$–$$$$
ZIMMER	6 Doppelzimmer im Haupthaus, 1 Chalet am See für 2 bis 4 Personen
KÜCHE	Internationale und traditionelle argentinische Küche
GESCHICHTE	Aus einer Ranch wurde ein Abenteuerspielplatz für Aktivurlauber
X-FAKTOR	Einer der besten Plätze fürs Fliegenfischen in Südamerika

ACCÈS	85 kilomètres au nord-west de l'aéroport de Bariloche
PRIX	$$$–$$$$
CHAMBRES	6 chambres doubles dans le bâtiment principal, 1 chalet au bord du lac pour 2 à 4 personnes
RESTAURATION	Cuisine argentine traditionnelle et internationale
HISTOIRE	Un ranch s'est transformé en terrain d'aventure pour touristes désirant des vacances actives
LES « PLUS »	L'un des meilleurs endroits pour la pêche au lancer dans toute l'Amérique du Sud

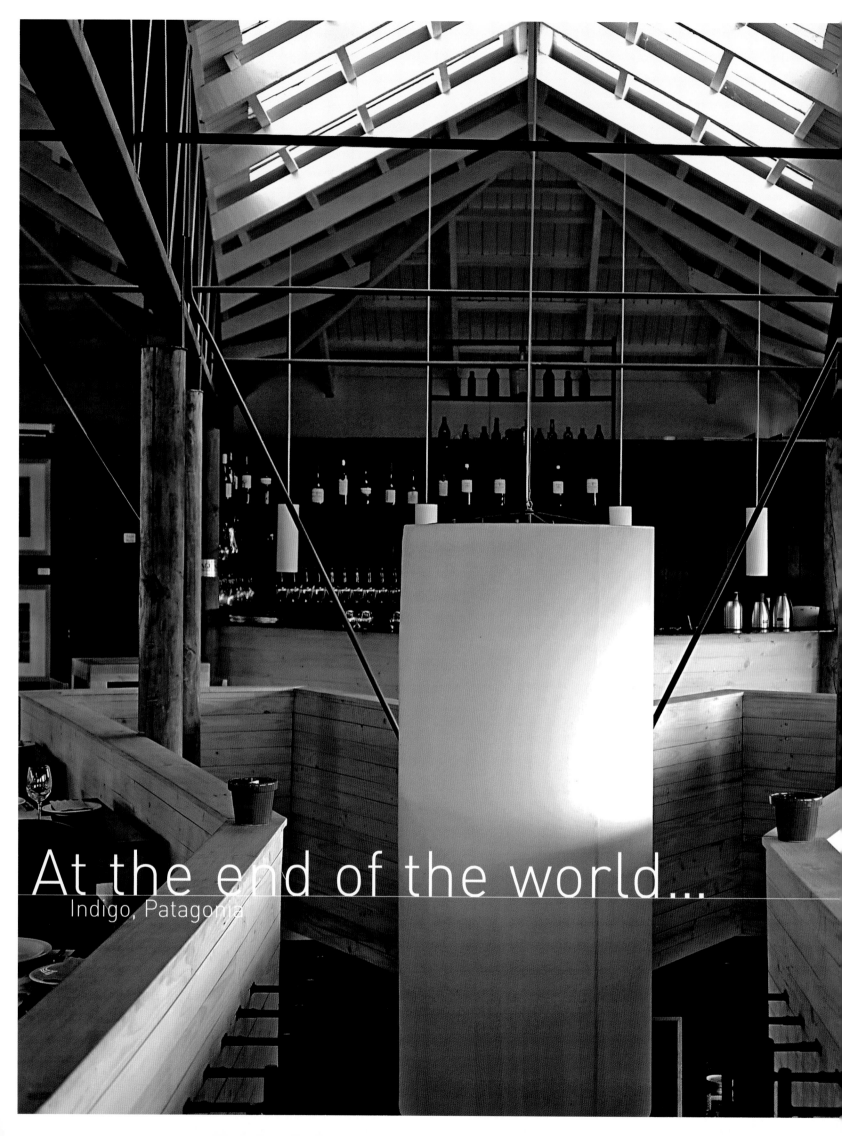

At the end of the world...
Indigo, Patagonia

Indigo, Patagonia

At the end of the world

In this hotel in southern Patagonia, the kind of luggage most often seen is a rucksack, of course, not a suitcase on wheels. It is precisely this mood of adventure that the Hotel Indigo conveys, with furnishings and architecture that have the character of an expedition camp. With ramps that lead through the building like mountain paths, numerous stairs and bridges, architect Sebastián Irarrazaval has made the hotel itself a bit of a challenge for arriving guests. For his avant-garde design at the end of the world he used materials typical of the place, such as wood and steel, and put the finishing touches to his work with fitting graphic design: the lettering on the façade, walls and doors is reminiscent of the shipping containers in the harbour. The great sense of freedom that is in the air here can be felt in every room: huge windows let in the outdoors, and while lying in bed guests can watch the interplay of clouds, wind and sky above Last Hope Sound. At the same time a feeling of being sheltered is generated – after all, people staying at a base camp want to have peace and recharge their batteries, perhaps in the jacuzzi or by taking a massage? And for organising the next tour, the hotel conveniently has its own desk available. Sometimes, however, the Indigo itself is the most exciting destination: with its mixed clientele of professional travellers and adventurers from all over the world, you can at any rate listen to the most amazing stories every evening in the bar over a glass of pisco sour.

Book to pack: "My Invented Country" by Isabel Allende

Indigo	
Ladrilleros 105	
Puerto Natales	
Patagonia	
Chile	
Tel: + 56 (61) 274 0671	
E-mail: info@indigopatagonia.com	
Website: www.indigopatagonia.com	

DIRECTIONS	Puerto Natales is situated on Last Hope Sound. There are direct flights from Santiago de Chile (the airport is five minutes from the hotel), or guests can fly to Punta Arenas, 250 km/160 miles southwest, for a pick-up there
RATES	$$
ROOMS	28 rooms and 1 suite
FOOD	Fish, beef and lamb from Patagonia, and fine French boulangerie goods
HISTORY	Immediately after it opened in 2006 the Indigo was seen as the hippest hotel in Puerto Natales, and since 2011 it has been part of the Noi hotel group
X-FACTOR	A princely pleasure: the open-air jacuzzis on the roof

Am Ende der Welt

In diesem Hotel im südlichen Patagonien ist natürlich der Rucksack das häufigste Reisegepäck und nicht der Rollkoffer. Und genau diesen Abenteuercharakter verströmt auch das Hotel Indigo, das mit seiner Einrichtung und seiner Architektur wie ein Expeditionslager wirkt. Mit Rampen, die wie Bergpfade durch das Gebäude führen, und vielen Treppen und Brücken hat Architekt Sebastián Irarrazaval das Haus selbst zu einer kleinen Herausforderung für die Ankommenden gemacht. Für sein Avantgarde-Design am Ende der Welt verwendete er ortstypische Materialien wie Holz und Stahl und krönte seine Arbeit mit einem stimmigen Grafikdesign: Die Beschriftungen von Fassade, Wänden und Türen erinnern an die der Schiffscontainer im Hafen. Die große Freiheit, die hier in der Luft liegt, spürt man auch in jedem Zimmer: Riesige Fenster lassen die Natur in die Räume, und man kann vom Bett aus dem Zusammenspiel von Wolken, Wind und Himmel über dem »Fjord of Last Hope« zusehen. Gleichzeitig wurde auch für Geborgenheit gesorgt, schließlich soll man in diesem Basislager auch wieder Ruhe und Kraft tanken können, vielleicht sogar im Whirlpool oder bei einer Massage? Und für die Organisation der nächsten Tour steht dann ganz bequem ein hoteleigener Schalter zur Verfügung. Manchmal ist aber auch das Indigo selbst das spannendste Ziel: Mit seinem bunten Publikum aus Reiseprofis und Abenteurern aus aller Welt hört man hier jeden Abend an der Bar bei einem Glas Pisco Sour jedenfalls die tollsten Geschichten.

Buchtipp: »Mein erfundenes Land« von Isabel Allende

Au bout du monde

Les voyageurs qui arrivent dans cet hôtel de Patagonie australe sont bien sûr le plus souvent équipés non pas de valises à roulettes, mais de sacs à dos. Et c'est précisément cette atmosphère d'aventure qui enveloppe aussi l'Hotel Indigo, dont l'architecture et l'aménagement intérieur évoquent un camp de base. Avec des rampes qui, tels des chemins de montagne, traversent le bâtiment ainsi qu'avec une multitude d'escaliers et de galeries de circulation, l'architecte Sebastián Irarrazaval soumet d'emblée les arrivants à une petite épreuve. Son architecture avant-gardiste à l'autre bout du monde est servie par des matériaux typiques du site, comme le bois et l'acier, et couronnée par un graphisme cohérent : les inscriptions sur la façade, les murs et les portes rappellent celles des conteneurs des bateaux que l'on voit dans le port. La grande liberté qui flotte ici dans l'air est palpable dans chaque chambre : la nature s'y invite par les immenses baies vitrées, et l'on peut observer depuis son lit le jeu des nuages et du vent dans le ciel au-dessus du « fjord de la dernière espérance ». Comme on doit pouvoir se reposer et refaire le plein d'énergie dans un camp de base, le bien-être n'est pas en reste, avec jacuzzis et massages. Et quand vient l'heure d'organiser l'excursion suivante, il suffit de consulter le spécialiste dans les murs mêmes de l'hôtel, encore que parfois Indigo soit lui-même la destination la plus fascinante : avec son public très mélangé de professionnels des voyages et d'aventuriers venus des quatre coins du monde, on entend chaque soir au bar les histoires les plus folles tout en prenant un verre de pisco sour.

Livre à emporter : « Mon pays réinventé » d'Isabel Allende

ANREISE	Am »Fjord der letzten Hoffnung« gelegen. Von Santiago de Chile gibt es Direktflüge dorthin (der Flughafen ist 5 Minuten vom Hotel entfernt), oder man fliegt ins 250 Kilometer südwestlich gelegene Punta Arenas und wird dort abgeholt
PREIS	$$
ZIMMER	28 Zimmer und 1 Suite
KÜCHE	Fisch, Rind und Lamm sowie französische Backwaren
GESCHICHTE	Gleich nach seiner Eröffnung im Jahr 2006 galt das Indigo als angesagtestes Hotel von Puerto Natales, seit 2011 gehört es zur Noi-Hotelgruppe
X-FAKTOR	Königliches Vergnügen: Open-Air-Jacuzzis auf dem Dach

ACCÈS	Situé dans le « fjord de la dernière espérance ». On prend un vol direct au départ de Santiago du Chili (l'aéroport est à 5 minutes de l'hôtel) ou un vol à destination de Punta Arenas, où l'on vient vous chercher
PRIX	$$
CHAMBRES	28 chambres et 1 suite
RESTAURATION	Poisson, bœuf et agneau de Patagonie ainsi que viennoiseries françaises
HISTOIRE	Peu de temps après son ouverture en 2006, l'Indigo était devenu l'hôtel où descendre à Puerto Natales. Membre de la chaîne hôtelière Noi depuis 2011
LES « PLUS »	Un traitement royal : les jacuzzis sur le toit

Room with a view...
Remota, Patagonia

Remota, Patagonia

Room with a view

Even from a distance it is apparent that the Remota cannot be a normal hotel. Like the roots of a great tree it has been fitted into the wild landscape of southern Patagonia, reaching out to the fjord with its head down, not attracting attention. When designing this hotel, which opened in 2005, architect Germán del Sol took his inspiration from the shapes of Patagonian animal shelters that offer protection from wind and weather. Behind the intriguing façade and beneath the grass-covered roof he has furnished bright rooms with furniture made from local lenga wood and fabrics in soft shades of yellow. The message is that a protective space awaits guests here, giving them a refuge when they return from their expeditions: because that is, after all, one of the main activities in Puerto Natales. This small fishing village in the south of Patagonia is an ideal base for hiking, bike and kayak tours, for example in the Torres del Paine National Park. Surrounded by all this natural beauty, a hotel can makes its mark with the simplest of offerings: warm-hearted service, lots of cosy spots with a fantastic view, and cuisine that combines the best from land and sea. Walkers can soothe their aching muscles in the outdoor jacuzzi while seeking out their destination for the following day. Sustainability is the most important rule of the house. The sods of grass that were removed to build the hotel were replanted on the roof, the construction materials all come from the region, and there's no point in looking for a television in the room. Just look through the window to tune in anytime to the best channel of all …

Book to pack: "Patagonia Express" by Luis Sepúlveda

Remota
Ruta 9 Norte, km 1.5
Huerto 279
Puerto Natales
Patagonia
Chile
Tel: + 56 (61) 241 4040 (hotel)
Tel: + 56 (2) 387 1500 (reservations)
E-mail: infoeu@remota.cl
Website: www.remotahotel.com

DIRECTIONS	From Santiago de Chile fly direct to Puerto Natales or to Punta Arenas 250 km southeast (free transfer from the airport to the hotel)
RATES	$$$$
ROOMS	72 rooms
FOOD	The ingredients for the hearty meals come from farms in the region
HISTORY	The spectacular building was opened in 2005
X-FACTOR	You can learn a lot about sustainable architecture

Zimmer mit Aussicht

Schon von Weitem sieht man dem Remota an, dass es kein gewöhnliches Hotel sein kann. Wie eine große Baumwurzel fügt es sich in die wilde Landschaft Südpatagoniens ein, geduckt und unauffällig streckt sich das Gebäude zum Fjord. Beim Entwurf für dieses 2005 eingeweihte Hotel ließ sich Architekt Germán del Sol von den Formen patagonischer Ställe inspirieren, die Schutz vor Wind und Wetter bieten. Hinter der faszinierenden Fassade und unter den grasbewachsenen Dächern hat er helle Räume mit Möbeln aus lokalem Lenga-Holz sowie Stoffen in sanften Gelbtönen eingerichtet. Botschaft: Hier wartet ein warmer Schutzraum, der seinen Gästen Unterschlupf bietet, wenn sie von ihren Expeditionen zurückkommen. Denn das ist in Puerto Natales nun mal eine der Hauptbeschäftigungen. Das kleine Fischerdorf im Süden Patagoniens eignet sich bestens als Ausflugsbasis für Wanderungen, Bike- und Kajaktouren, zum Beispiel in den Torres-del-Paine-Nationalpark. Als Hotel kann man bei so viel Naturschönheit mit ganz einfachen Sachen punkten: Herzlichem Service, vielen gemütlichen Plätzen mit toller Aussicht und mit einer Küche, die das Beste aus Meer und Land vereint. Den Muskelkater können die Wanderer im Outdoor-Jacuzzi bekämpfen und dabei schon die Ziele für den nächsten Tag ins Auge nehmen. Nachhaltigkeit ist hier die wichtigste Hausregel – die Grasnarben, die beim Bau entfernt wurden, wurden auf dem Dach wieder angepflanzt, die Baumaterialien stammen alle aus der Region, und einen Fernseher sucht man im Zimmer vergeblich. Das beste Programm läuft eben immer hinter dem Fenster ...

Buchtipp: »Patagonien Express« von Luis Sepúlveda

Chambre avec vue

De loin, on voit déjà que le Remota ne peut pas être un hôtel comme les autres. Telle une immense racine d'arbre, la construction se fond dans le paysage sauvage de la Patagonie australe et avance vers le fjord en toute humilité et toute discrétion. Germán del Sol, l'architecte de cet hôtel inauguré en 2005, a repris le langage formel des hangars de Patagonie, qui protègent les bovins et les ovins des intempéries. L'étonnante façade et les toits végétalisés abritent des pièces lumineuses dont l'aménagement intérieur fait la part belle au lemba, bois d'œuvre local, et à des tissus dans des tons de jaune pâle. Le message est clair : un refuge chaleureux attend les visiteurs à leur retour d'expéditions, l'une des principales activités qu'offre Puerto Natales. Ce petit village de pêcheurs en Patagonie australe est un excellent camp de base pour entreprendre des randonnées à pied, à vélo et en kayak, notamment dans le parc national Torres del Paine. Dans pareil environnement naturel, un hôtel peut marquer des points avec des choses toutes simples : un service chaleureux, de nombreux endroits confortables avec une vue magnifique et une cuisine qui réunit le meilleur de la mer et de la terre. Les randonneurs peuvent régler leur compte à leurs courbatures dans le jacuzzi à ciel ouvert, tout en envisageant déjà les objectifs pour le lendemain. La durabilité est le maître-mot dans cet établissement : la couche gazonnée qu'il a fallu dégager pour les travaux a été réimplantée sur le toit, les matériaux de construction proviennent tous de la région et c'est en vain qu'on cherche un téléviseur dans sa chambre. Il est vrai que le plus beau spectacle se joue de l'autre côté de la vitre...

Livre à emporter : « Le Dernier Voyage du Patagonia Express » de Luis Sepúlveda

ANREISE	Von Santiago de Chile aus fliegt man direkt nach Puerto Natales oder ins 250 Kilometer südöstlich gelegene Punta Arenas (kostenloser Transfer vom Flughafen zum Hotel)
PREIS	$$$$
ZIMMER	72 Zimmer
KÜCHE	Die Zutaten für die herzhaften Gerichte liefern die Bauernhöfe der Region
GESCHICHTE	Das spektakuläre Haus wurde 2005 eröffnet
X-FAKTOR	Man kann viel über nachhaltige Architektur lernen

ACCÈS	On prend un vol direct au départ de Santiago du Chili (l'aéroport est à 5 minutes de l'hôtel) ou un vol à destination de Punta Arenas (transfert gratuit de l'aéroport à l'hôtel)
PRIX	$$$$
CHAMBRES	72 chambres
RESTAURATION	Les ingrédients des plats rustiques proviennent des fermes de la région
HISTOIRE	Cet établissement spectaculaire a ouvert ses portes en 2005
LES « PLUS »	Une belle leçon d'architecture durable

Patagonia and nothing but...
explora Patagonia, Patagonia

explora Patagonia, Patagonia

Patagonia and nothing but

It is the end of the world. A raw, rugged landscape where once colonial powers competed for the upper hand, and whalers and sealers made a living out of their bloody pursuit. But it is also country of almost unreal beauty: Patagonia, in southern Chile. Rarely will your lungs breathe so bracing an air. Rarely will you see such emerald-green lakes or such breathtaking mountain chains. In the very heart of the region is the Torres del Paine National Park, a region of granite needles, glacial waters, forests, and vast mosses, which is under UNESCO protection. It was there that explora Hotels opened their first establishment in 1993, the explora Patagonia, which looks very much as if it were an immense liner lying at anchor on the shoreline of Lago Pehoé. Chilean designer Germán del Sol has cast the architecture in an entirely marine mould, with a wood-cladding façade, a landing stage, a reception area resembling a cabin, and model ships in the lobby. As on a ship's deck, the rooms lie along seemingly endless passageways, and are fitted out in natural materials such as wood, hides, or stone. The philosophy of the house calls for purist quality, as evidenced in accessories such as hand-woven bed linen, rough-cut cakes of soap in the bathroom, or an entire ham on the breakfast buffet – it is an experience that involves all the senses and affords the purest encounter with nature. This is also true of the bathhouse with its panoramic view of the lake and mountains, and of the expeditions on offer every day – when professional guides lead visitors into the secret heart of Patagonia.

Book to pack: "Burning Patience" by Antonio Skármeta

explora Patagonia
Sector Salto Chico S/N
Comuna Torres del Paine
Casilia 57, Puerto Natales
Patagonia
Chile
Tel: + 56 (2) 2395 2580
E-mail: cthorsoe@explora.com
Website: www.explora.com

DIRECTIONS	Situated 200 km/125 miles northwest of Punta Arenas (domestic flights from Santiago). Transfer by minibus is organised
RATES	$$$$
ROOMS	49 rooms and suites
FOOD	First-rate, purist cuisine using fresh fish, vegetables, and fruit. There is also a bar
HISTORY	Opened in October 1993
X-FACTOR	Discover the end of the world!

Patagonien pur

Es ist das Ende der Welt; eine raue Landschaft, in der einst Kolonialmächte um die Vorherrschaft stritten und Wal- und Robbenjäger mit blutigen Methoden um ihren Lebensunterhalt kämpften – doch es ist auch eine Landschaft von fast unwirklicher Schönheit: Patagonien im Süden Chiles. Selten atmet man eine so kristallklare Luft wie hier, blickt auf smaragdgrün schimmernde Seen und auf Bergketten wie überdimensionale Fototapeten. Im Herzen dieser Region liegt der Nationalpark Torres del Paine, von der UNESCO geschützt und geprägt von Granitnadeln, Gletscherwasser, Wäldern sowie Moosflächen. Hier haben die explora Hotels 1993 ihr erstes Haus eröffnet: das explora Patagonia, das wie ein riesiger Dampfer am Ufer des Lago Pehoé vor Anker zu liegen scheint. Der chilenische Designer Germán del Sol setzt ganz auf eine bootartige Architektur – mit einer holzverkleideten Fassade, einem Zutrittssteg, einer kajütenähnlichen Rezeption und Schiffsmodellen in der Halle. Wie auf einem Deck liegen die Zimmer entlang scheinbar endloser Flure und sind mit natürlichen Materialien wie Holz, Fell oder Stein eingerichtet. Dass die Philosophie des Hauses der edle Purismus ist, merkt man an Accessoires wie handgewebter Bettwäsche, groben Seifenstücken im Bad oder einem ganzen Schinken auf dem Frühstücksbuffet – hier soll man alle Sinne einsetzen und die Natur in ihrer reinsten Form erleben. Das gilt auch für Besuche im Badehaus mit Panoramablick auf See und Berge sowie für die Expeditionen, die jeden Tag angeboten werden – geführt von professionellen Guides kommen die Gäste so den Geheimnissen Patagoniens auf die Spur.
Buchtipp: »Mit brennender Geduld« von Antonio Skármeta

Purisme en Patagonie

La Patagonie, c'est au bout du monde, une terre sauvage qui a vu les luttes d'influence entre les puissances coloniales et les chasseurs de baleines et de phoques se battre pour survivre dans un environnement aussi rude qu'eux. Mais sa beauté est presque irréelle. L'air y est d'une pureté cristalline, les lacs chatoient, couleur d'émeraude, au pied de la cordillère spectaculaire. C'est au cœur de cette région que se trouve le parc national Torres del Paine, protégé par l'UNESCO, avec ses tours granitiques, ses glaciers, ses chutes d'eau, ses forêts et sa steppe. En 1993, la chaîne explora Hotels a ouvert ici son premier hôtel, l'explora Patagonia, qui semble amarré, tel un gigantesque vapeur, sur les rives du Lago Pehoé. Le designer chilien Germán del Sol a misé sur une architecture navale – façade habillée de bois, passerelle, « cabine » de réception – et décoré le hall de maquettes de bateau. Les chambres, disposées comme sur un pont dans de longs corridors, sont décorées de matériaux naturels comme le bois, la fourrure ou la pierre. L'ambiance est imprégnée de purisme, on le remarque par exemple dans la literie tissée à la main, les morceaux de savon « grossiers » dans la salle de bains ou le jambon entier que propose le buffet du petit-déjeuner. Ici, tous les sens doivent entrer en action et percevoir la nature sous sa forme la plus pure. Le même souci de noble simplicité règne dans la maison de bains qui offre un panorama splendide sur le lac et les montagnes ainsi que sur les expéditions proposées tous les jours. Accompagnés par des guides professionnels, les hôtes s'en vont percer les mystères de la Patagonie.
Livre à emporter : « Une ardente patience » de Antonio Skármeta

ANREISE	200 Kilometer nordwestlich von Punta Arenas gelegen (dorthin Inlandsflüge ab Santiago), Transfer im Minibus wird organisiert
PREIS	$$$$
ZIMMER	49 Zimmer und Suiten
KÜCHE	Erstklassig und ebenfalls dem Purismus verpflichtet – mit frischem Fisch, Gemüse und Obst. Außerdem eine Bar
GESCHICHTE	Im Oktober 1993 eröffnet
X-FAKTOR	Entdecken Sie das Ende der Welt!

ACCÈS	Situé à 200 kilomètres au nord-ouest de Punta Arenas (là-bas, vols intérieurs à partir de Santiago), un transfert en minibus est organisé
PRIX	$$$$
CHAMBRES	49 chambres et suites
RESTAURATION	De premier choix, avec également des accents puristes – poisson frais, légumes et fruits. Et un bar
HISTOIRE	Ouvert depuis octobre 1993
LES « PLUS »	Pour découvrir le bout du monde !

A question of style...
Hotel Antumalal, Araucanía

Hotel Antumalal, Araucanía

A question of style

In October 1938 a young couple fleeing the Nazis, Guillermo and Catalina Pollak from Prague, arrived in Pucón with dreams of making a new life for themselves in Chile. But at first their chosen home at the other side of the world proved full of obstacles. A volcanic eruption and a fire destroyed the Pollakstet club and hotel. Ten years later, however, all was well and things were on the up at last – literally so. High on a rocky plateau above Lake Villarrica, together with Chilean architect Jorge Elton, the couple created what has remained to this day one of the most unusual hotels in all South America: a long, flat building in the Bauhaus style. Antumalal ("sunshine court" in the language of the Mapuche people) commands views across a garden of flowers, far across the water, to the volcano, the snow-capped summit of which looks as if it had been powdered with icing sugar. The view from the panoramic windows is far better than any movie. The design focusses on native wood and Chilean country style; every room has its own fireplace as standard. An entertaining mixture of Czech and South American dishes is served in the restaurant, and the proprietors are especially proud of their bar counter, which measures 3.99 metres (about 13 feet) and was fashioned from a single piece of timber. The splendid Chilean wines should not be over-indulged in, though – it would be a pity to spoil your delight in nearby Huerquehue National Park by visiting with a hangover!

Book to pack: "Memoirs" by Pablo Neruda

Hotel Antumalal	
Km 2 Camino Pucón – Villarrica	
Pucón	
Chile	
Tel: + 56 (45) 244 1011 and 244 1012	
E-mail: info@antumalal.com	
Website: www.antumalal.com	

DIRECTIONS	90 km/56 miles from the main Temuco airport, which is reached by domestic flight from Santiago. 90-minute transfer to hotel on request
RATES	$$
ROOMS	11 double rooms, 1 suite, 1 family suite, 1 royal chalet
FOOD	"Restaurant del Parque" serving Czech-Chilean cuisine. Also, "Don Guillermo's Bar"
HISTORY	Opened in 1950, the hotel was built in the Bauhaus style
X-FACTOR	Unique architecture, unique views

Eine Frage des Stils

Es war im Oktober 1938, als Guillermo und Catalina Pollak aus Prag nach Pucón kamen – ein junges Ehepaar auf der Flucht vor den Nazis und voller Träume von einem neuen Leben in Chile. Doch die Wahlheimat am anderen Ende der Welt lag anfangs voller Stolpersteine: Ein Vulkanausbruch und ein Feuer zerstörten den Club und das Hotel, das die Pollaks betrieben. Aber nach zehn Jahren ging es endlich aufwärts – im wahrsten Sinne des Wortes: Auf einem Felsplateau hoch über dem Villarrica-See entwarfen die beiden gemeinsam mit dem chilenischen Architekten Jorge Elton eines der damals wie heute ungewöhnlichsten Hotels in Südamerika: ein flaches, lang gezogenes Gebäude im Bauhausstil. Antumalal (»Sonnenhof« in der Sprache der Mapuche) blickt auf einen blühenden Garten, weit über das Wasser und bis zum Vulkan, dessen schneebedeckte Kuppe wie mit Puderzucker bestreut wirkt. Die Sicht aus den Panoramafenstern der Zimmer schlägt jeden Blockbuster. Das Design konzentriert sich auf einheimisches Holz und chilenischen Countrystil; ein eigener Kamin gehört in jedem Raum zum Standard. Eine amüsante Mischung aus tschechischen und südamerikanischen Gerichten wird im Restaurant serviert, und besonders stolz sind die Inhaber auf ihren Bartresen, der 3,99 Meter lang ist und aus einem einzigen Holzstück geschliffen wurde. Zu viel chilenischen Wein sollte man hier allerdings nicht bestellen – mit Kopfschmerzen wären die Exkursionen in den nahen Huerquehue National Park nur halb so eindrucksvoll.

Buchtipp: »Ich bekenne, ich habe gelebt« von Pablo Neruda

Question de style

Jeune couple fuyant Prague et les nazis, Guillermo et Catalina Pollak sont arrivés à Pucón au Chili, en octobre 1938, avec le rêve d'une vie meilleure. Néanmoins, ce pays du bout du monde leur réservait aussi d'autres écueils, d'ordre naturel cette fois : le club et l'hôtel qu'ils exploitaient au début ont été détruits par une éruption volcanique et un incendie. Enfin, au bout de dix ans, ils ont vu leurs efforts récompensés. Sur un plateau rocheux au-dessus du lac Villarrica, Guillermo et Catalina Pollak ont conçu en collaboration avec l'architecte chilien Jorge Elton ce qui est resté à ce jour l'un des hôtels les plus insolites d'Amérique latine et se présente comme une construction longue et basse de style Bauhaus. Antumalal (« cour du soleil » en mapuche) se dresse au-dessus d'un jardin fleuri, il surplombe la mer et regarde au loin le volcan dont la cime enneigée a l'air saupoudrée de sucre glace. On délaisserait le meilleur film à succès pour jouir de la vue depuis les fenêtres panoramiques. Le design est concentré sur les essences locales et le style rustique chilien ; chaque chambre possède une cheminée. La cuisine servie ici est un mélange amusant de spécialités tchèques et sud-américaines, et les propriétaires sont particulièrement fiers de leur bar de 3,99 mètres taillé dans un seul tronc d'arbre. Toutefois, attention à la migraine, celui qui veut partir frais et dispos en excursion au Huerquehue National Park tout proche veillera à consommer les vins chiliens avec modération.

Livre à emporter : « J'avoue que j'ai vécu » de Pablo Neruda

ANREISE	90 Kilometer vom Flughafen Temuco entfernt (dorthin Inlandsflüge ab Santiago). 90-minütiger Transfer zum Hotel auf Wunsch
PREIS	$$
ZIMMER	11 Doppelzimmer, 1 Suite, 1 Family Suite, 1 Royal Chalet
KÜCHE	»Restaurant del Parque« mit tschechisch-chilenischer Küche. Außerdem »Don Guillermo's Bar«
GESCHICHTE	1950 eröffnet, im Bauhausstil erbaut
X-FAKTOR	Einzigartige Architektur, einzigartige Aussicht

ACCÈS	Situé à 90 kilomètres de l'aéroport de Temuco (vols intérieurs à partir de Santiago). Transfert de 90 minutes sur demande
PRIX	$$
CHAMBRES	11 chambres doubles, 1 suite, 1 Family Suite, 1 Royal Chalet
RESTAURATION	Cuisine tchéco-chilienne au « Restaurant del Parque ». Et le « Don Guillermo's Bar »
HISTOIRE	Se style Bauhaus, ouvert depuis 1950
LES « PLUS »	Architecture unique, panorama unique

A summer residence in the so

Hotel Casa Real, Región Metropolitana

uth...

Hotel Casa Real, Región Metropolitana

A summer residence in the south

When Domingo Fernández Concha established the Santa Rita winery in 1880, his aim for the future was not only to grow some of Chile's best wines – he also wanted to live in one of the nation's finest houses. So he had a luxury country residence built south of Santiago, in the Pompeian style, with majestic flights of steps, slender pillars, and high windows. He resided beneath richly ornamented wooden ceilings and crystal chandeliers, viewed his reflection in gilt-framed mirrors, and hung gleaming oil paintings on his walls. He even had a billiards table imported from Great Britain. And all of this grand style can be savoured to this day; for in 1996 the house became the Hotel Casa Real, offering guests a veritable journey into the past. Indeed, the grounds laid out in 1882 by French landscape architect Guillermo Renner may well be even finer than they originally were, having matured into an enchanting estate with century-old cedars, almond, olive, and lemon trees, and what may well be the largest bougainvillea on the entire continent. The hotel also has the Doña Paula Restaurant, named after the former owner, and an homage to Chile's independence hero Bernardo O'Higgins and his 120 soldiers, who sought refuge here after a fight with the Spanish. The finest products of the estate all carry "120" in their names, as in "120 Chardonnay" or "120 Sauvignon Blanc". Both are in fact among the best Chilean wines – just as Domingo Fernández Concha once hoped they would be.

Book to pack: "The House of the Spirits" by Isabel Allende

Hotel Casa Real

Viña Santa Rita, Av. Padre Hurtado 0695

Alto Jahuel/Buin

Chile

Tel: + 56 (2) 2821 9966

E-mail: receptionhotel@santarita.com

Website: www.santarita.com

DIRECTIONS	Situated 25 km/15 miles south of Santiago
RATES	$$
ROOMS	10 double rooms, 6 suites
FOOD	The "Doña Paula" Restaurant serves very good regional and international cuisine. An excellent wine list, including the estate's own range of wines
HISTORY	The property, dating from 1880, converted into a country hotel in 1996
X-FACTOR	Lead the life of a wine-grower – on a choice estate

Sommersitz im Süden

Als Domingo Fernández Concha 1880 das Weingut Santa Rita gründete, ging es ihm nicht nur darum, hier künftig einige der besten Weine Chiles anzubauen – er wollte auch in einem der schönsten Häuser der Nation wohnen. Südlich von Santiago ließ er ein Landhaus de luxe errichten; im pompejanischen Stil, mit prachtvollen Freitreppen, schlanken Säulen und hohen Fenstern. Er residierte unter reich verzierten Holzdecken und Kristalllüstern, blickte in goldumrahmte Spiegel und auf glänzende Ölgemälde – und besaß sogar einen aus England importierten Billardtisch. All das hochherrschaftliche Flair kann man noch heute genießen, denn seit 1996 ist das Haus das Hotel Casa Real und lädt seine Gäste zu einer Reise in die Vergangenheit ein. Vielleicht noch schöner als anno dazumal ist der Park rund um das Anwesen, den der französische Landschaftsarchitekt Guillermo Renner 1882 anlegte – ein verwunschenes Fleckchen Erde mit jahrhundertealten Zedern, Mandel-, Oliven- und Zitronenbäumen sowie der wahrscheinlich größten Bougainvillea des Kontinents. Zum Hotel gehört außerdem das Restaurant Doña Paula, benannt nach seiner ehemaligen Eigentümerin und eine Hommage an Chiles Unabhängigkeitsheld Bernardo O'Higgins und seine 120 Soldaten, die hier nach einer Schlacht gegen die Spanier Unterschlupf suchten. Die besten Produkte des Hauses tragen alle ein »120« im Namen, zum Beispiel der »120 Chardonnay« oder der »120 Sauvignon Blanc«. Beide gehören übrigens zu den besten Weinen Chiles – ganz im Sinne von Domingo Fernández Concha.

Buchtipp: »Das Geisterhaus« von Isabel Allende

La magie du Sud

Lorsque Domingo Fernández Concha a fondé le vignoble de Santa Rita en 1880, il ne voulait pas seulement produire ici quelques-uns des meilleurs vins du Chili. Il avait aussi l'intention d'habiter dans l'une des plus belles maisons du pays. Il fit édifier au sud de Santiago une villa luxueuse de style pompéien, dotée de magnifiques perrons, de colonnes élancées et de hautes fenêtres. Les salons abritaient des plafonds lambrissés richement décorés et des lustres de cristal, des miroirs aux cadres dorés, des tableaux peints à l'huile – et même un billard importé d'Angleterre. Cette ambiance aristocratique existe toujours. Devenue l'Hotel Casa Real en 1996, la maison invite ses hôtes à voyager dans le temps et à goûter les plaisirs d'une époque disparue. Le parc agencé en 1882 par le paysagiste français Guillermo Renner est peut-être encore plus beau qu'alors. C'est un endroit magique qui abrite des cèdres, des amandiers, des oliviers et des citronniers séculaires ainsi que probablement le plus grand bougainvillée du continent. Le Doña Paula Restaurant fait partie de l'hôtel. Il doit son nom à son ancienne propriétaire et rend hommage au héros de l'indépendance chilienne Bernardo O'Higgins et à ses 120 soldats qui vinrent se réfugier ici après une bataille contre les troupes espagnoles. Les meilleurs produits de la maison sont tous nommés « 120 » en l'honneur de ces patriotes, par exemple le « 120 Chardonnay » ou le « 120 Sauvignon Blanc ». Ces deux là font partie des meilleurs vins du Chili – Domingo Fernández Concha peut donc dormir tranquille.

Livre à emporter : « La maison aux esprits » d'Isabel Allende

ANREISE	25 Kilometer südlich von Santiago gelegen		ACCÈS	Situé à 25 kilomètres au sud de Santiago
PREIS	$$		PRIX	$$
ZIMMER	10 Doppelzimmer, 6 Suiten		CHAMBRES	10 chambres doubles, 6 suites
KÜCHE	Restaurant »Doña Paula« mit sehr guter regionaler und internationaler Küche. Ausgezeichnete Weinkarte, hauseigene Vinothek		RESTAURATION	Le « Doña Paula » Restaurant propose une savoureuse cuisine régionale et internationale. Remarquable carte des vins, la maison a sa propre cave
GESCHICHTE	Anwesen aus dem Jahr 1880, 1996 Umbau zum Landhotel		HISTOIRE	Domaine datant de 1880, transformé en hôtel de campagne en 1996
X-FAKTOR	Wohnen wie ein Winzer – auf einem der besten Weingüter		LES « PLUS »	Célébrer la « dive bouteille » dans l'un des meilleurs domaines viticoles

Schlicht schön

Die Landschaft unter dem weiß schraffierten Himmel ist eine der kargsten und trockensten der Erde – und dennoch eine der faszinierendsten. Die Atacamawüste im Norden Chiles besitzt den rund 300 Quadratkilometer bedeckenden Salzsee Salar de Atacama, der gewaltige Lithiumreserven birgt und Heimat der rosafarbenen Flamingos ist. Sie bietet geheimnisvolle Vulkane, die geübte Bergsteiger sogar bezwingen können, die Tatio-Geysire, die jeden Morgen Wasserfontänen in die Luft fauchen – und nicht zuletzt das Hotel explora Atacama. Der chilenische Architekt Germán del Sol hat es auf 2.400 Metern Höhe am Rand des Oasendorfs San Pedro de Atacama gebaut und mit einem Haupthaus und drei Höfen wie eine Farm konzipiert. Fern aller gewohnten Zivilisation bietet es jeden Komfort, spiegelt aber zugleich die Klarheit und Schlichtheit der umliegenden Landschaft wider. Einfache Rampen und Treppen verbinden die Patios und die Gebäude, große Fensterfronten geben den Blick auf die Wüste frei (sogar vom Bett aus bietet sich ein zauberhaftes Panorama), und die Zimmer sind mit regionalen Materialien wie schwarzem Naturstein ausgestattet. Die milden Temperaturen genießt man bei Tagesausflügen, an den vier lang gezogenen und schnörkellos designten Pools, bei Massagen in der »Casa del Agua« oder in den 30 Kilometer entfernten »Termas de Puritama«, den heißen Quellen auf 3.100 Metern Höhe. Nachts holt das Hotel seinen Gästen dann die Sterne vom Himmel: Von der neuen Plattform »Pueblo de Estrellas« aus kann man mithilfe dreier Teleskope einen Blick in den Himmel über der Wüste werfen, der wie schwarzblauer Samt voller glitzernder Pailletten wirkt.

Buchtipp: »Das Abenteuer des Miguel Littín« von Gabriel García Márquez

Tout simplement beau

Le paysage qui s'étend sous le ciel strié de blanc est l'un des plus pauvres et des plus arides de la Terre, et pourtant il est aussi l'un des plus fascinants. C'est sur ce désert d'Atacama, dans le nord du Chili, que se trouve le lac salé, Salar de Atacama, d'une surface de 300 kilomètres carrés, à la fois une énorme réserve de lithium et un refuge pour les flamands roses. Le désert offre aussi ses volcans mystérieux que peuvent escalader des alpinistes expérimentés, ses geysers Tatio qui crachent tous les matins des fontaines d'eau dans les airs – et, last but not least, l'hôtel explora Atacama. L'architecte chilien Germán del Sol l'a construit à 2 400 mètres d'altitude près du village de San Pedro de Atacama et l'a conçu comme un ranch avec un bâtiment principal et trois annexes. Loin de toute civilisation, il offre beaucoup de confort tout en reflétant la clarté et la sobriété du paysage environnant. Des rampes et des escaliers tout simples relient les patios et les bâtiments, des fenêtres panoramiques donnent sur le désert (on a même une vue splendide de son lit) et les chambres sont décorées avec des matériaux de la région, comme la pierre noire. On profitera des températures agréables pour faire des excursions d'une journée, pour se baigner dans l'un des quatre longs bassins, pour se faire masser dans la « Casa del Agua » ou encore pour se rendre aux « Termas de Puritama », des sources chaudes situées à trente kilomètres de l'hôtel, à 3 100 mètres d'altitude. La nuit, l'hôtel fait descendre les étoiles du ciel tout spécialement pour ses clients : sur la nouvelle plate-forme « Pueblo de Estrellas », on peut ainsi à l'aide de trois télescopes regarder le ciel au-dessus du désert qui ressemble alors à du satin bleu foncé parsemé de paillettes étincelantes.

Livre à emporter : « L'aventure de Miguel Littín, clandestin au Chili » de Gabriel García Márquez

ANREISE	100 Kilometer südöstlich von Calama gelegen (dorthin regelmäßige Flugverbindungen ab Santiago de Chile). Einstündiger Bustransfer wird organisiert
PREIS	$$$$
ZIMMER	50 Doppelzimmer
KÜCHE	Gesunde Küche mit vorwiegend regionalen Produkten. Mittags und abends stehen jeweils zwei Menüs zur Auswahl
GESCHICHTE	Am 1. September 1998 eröffnet
X-FAKTOR	Den Geheimnissen der Wüste auf der Spur

ACCÈS	Situé à 100 kilomètres au sud-est de Calama (vols réguliers depuis Santiago de Chile). Le transfert d'une heure en car est organisé
PRIX	$$$$
CHAMBRES	50 chambres doubles
RESTAURATION	Cuisine saine préparée surtout avec des produits de la région. Deux menus au choix le midi et le soir
HISTOIRE	Ouvert depuis le 1er septembre 1998
LES « PLUS »	Sur les traces des mystères du désert

Awasi, Atacama

More than five stars

The first thing that guests talk about when they have returned from their stay is the stars. This is not a hotel category, but the amazing sky that extends above them at night. The dryness of the region, the high altitude and many cloud-free nights make San Pedro de Atacama a paradise for fans of astronomy and romantics. That is why architect Gonzalo Domínguez and his family built their Hotel Awasi ("at home") in 2006 exactly here in this oasis. Inspired by traditional building methods, they worked only with local stone, earth and wood. The interior, too, is from this region – from the custom-made furniture to the handmade dolls. Outside, a world of extremes awaits: the world's driest desert has a distinct, sublime beauty with an atmosphere all of its own. The rugged mountain ranges, salt pans, lagoons and volcanoes beneath a turquoise sky are unforgettable. Guests can take Jeep tours through the salt desert or visit the hot springs of Puritama. The Awasi with its restrained design is ideal for digesting the impressions gained during the day in peace and quiet. Antiques typical of Chile and colourful fabrics help body and soul to relax, and the cosy reading lounge is a good place to philosophise about the vast extent of the desert. In the evenings a warmly crackling campfire is lit, and over a glass of excellent Chilean wine, guests wait for the show of stars that will shortly appear in the wide night sky.

Book to pack: "Canto General" by Pablo Neruda

Awasi	
Tocopilla 4	
San Pedro de Atacama	
Antofagasta	
Chile	
Tel: + 56 (55) 851 460/2233 9641	
E-mail: info@awasi.cl	
Website: www.awasi.cl	

DIRECTIONS	San Pedro de Atacama lies at an altitude of 2,400 m/ 7,900 ft, 1,670 km/1,040 miles north of Santiago de Chile. The nearest airport, at Calama, is 96 km/60 miles away
RATES	$$$$
ROOMS	10 cottages for 2 persons each
FOOD	Delicious Chilean and international meals. Everything is homemade; even the bread is baked in-house
HISTORY	The San Pedro oasis has been settled since early times. A historic wall surrounds the Awasi, which opened in 2006
X-FACTOR	The pleasantest spot for observing the clearest night sky in the world is the pool

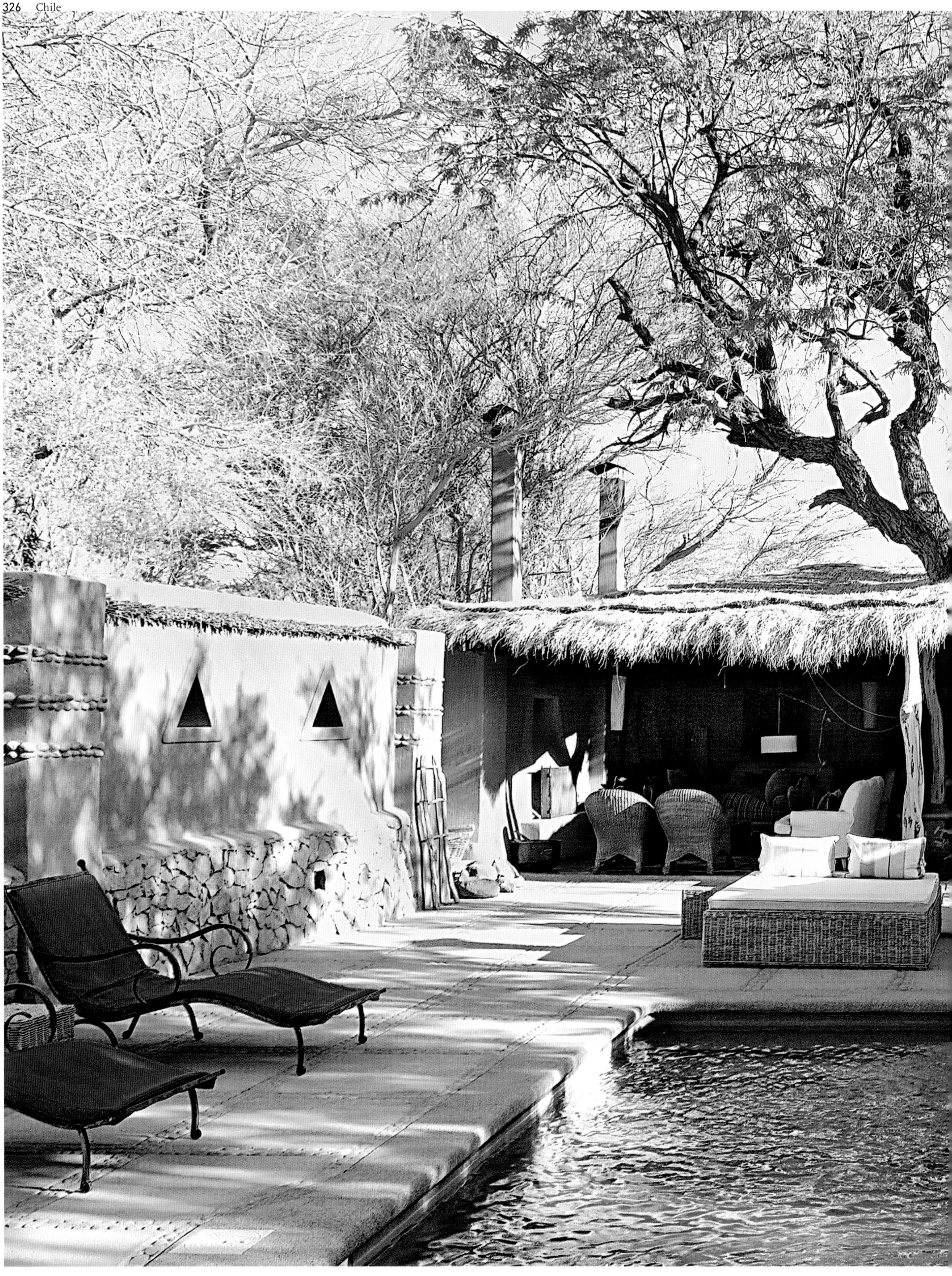

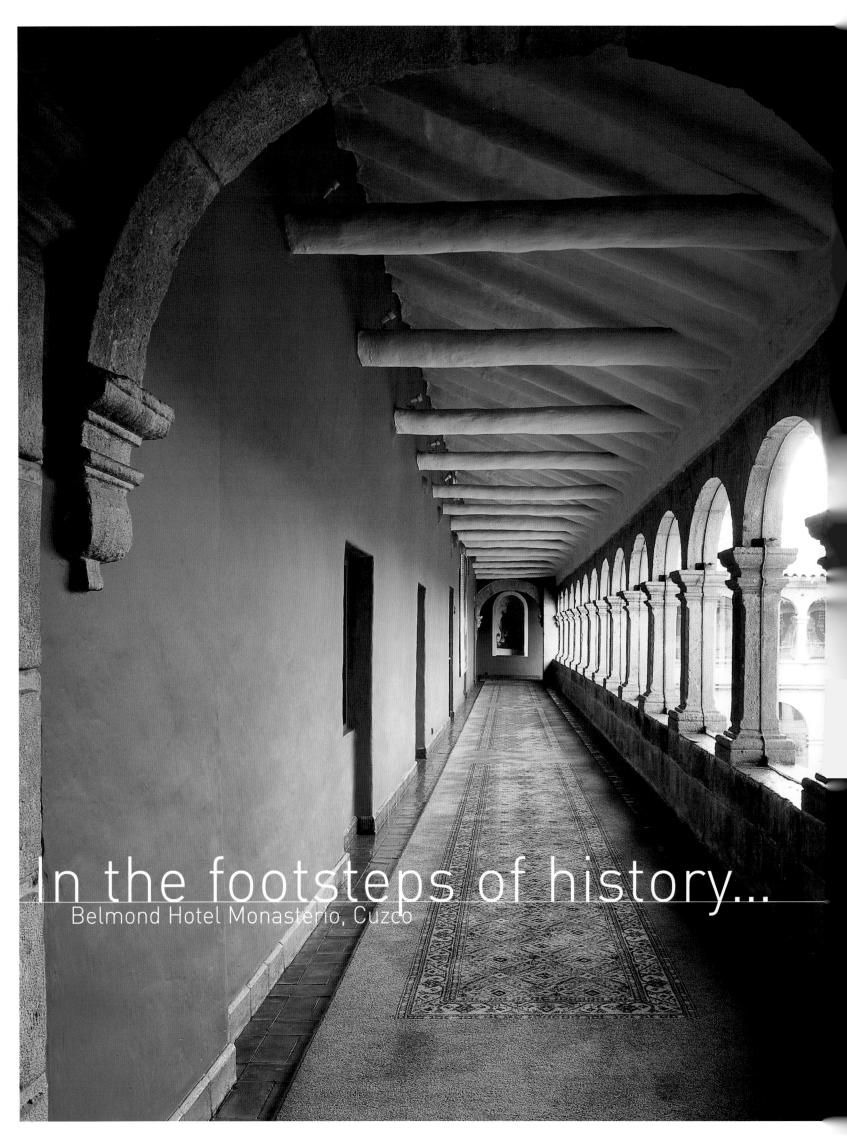

In the footsteps of history...
Belmond Hotel Monasterio, Cuzco

Belmond Hotel Monasterio, Cuzco

In the footsteps of history

In the 15th century, when the Incas put up the first buildings in Cuzco, they were not founding anything so humble as a mere capital. Cuzco was their holy site, and the very centre of their universe. The city retained its pride in the years of Spanish colonial rule, and now, with a place on the UNESCO World Heritage schedule, it is one of South America's most important and diverse cities. If you want to savour history to the full here, at an altitude of 3,300 metres (over 10,000 feet) and with the Andes affording a stupendous backdrop, the Belmond Hotel Monasterio is the place to stay. Built in 1592 as a monastery, it is perhaps the loveliest habitable museum in all Peru – the venerable walls within which you dwell are so thick, it's as if you needed protecting from the outside world. When you walk beneath the rounded arches of the cloisters, it can almost come as a disappointment not to encounter a monk around the next corner. The ground plan of the former monastic cells, shared halls and chapel has remained largely unaltered – but the spartan appointments are a thing of the past. No two rooms in the Belmond Hotel Monasterio are alike. In one you sit on a majestic deep-plush armchair; in another hangs a splendid gilt-framed painting. There are costly antiques, gleaming mirrors and crystal chandeliers. From cable television to mini-bars, the rooms have every modern comfort, and now even offer an enriched oxygen supply for those who may suffer from altitude sickness. After a night in the Monasterio's "oxygen tent" you'll have no problems enjoying the magic of Cuzco or taking the trip to Machu Picchu – the "lost city of the Incas" is just a three-and-a-half-hour train ride away.

Book to pack: "Death in the Andes" by Mario Vargas Llosa

Belmond Hotel Monasterio	DIRECTIONS	Located in the heart of Cuzco, 10 min. from the airport
Calle Palacio 136, Plazoleta Nazarenas	RATES	$$$–$$$$
Cuzco	ROOMS	26 superior rooms, 78 deluxe rooms, 15 junior suites, 4 presidential suites, 2 royal suites
Peru		
Tel: + 51 (84) 604 000	FOOD	2 restaurants serving Peruvian and international cuisine. The most attractive is "El Tupay" with its festive Inca Dinner
Fax: + 51 (84) 604 001		
E-mail: perures.fits@belmond.com	HISTORY	Built in 1592 as a monastery, a hotel since 1995
Website: www.belmond.com	X-FACTOR	History at close quarters

Wandeln auf historischen Wegen

Als die Inka im 15. Jahrhundert die ersten Häuser von Cuzco errichteten, gründeten sie weit mehr als eine einfache Hauptstadt – Cuzco war ihr Heiligtum und das Zentrum ihrer Welt. Die Stadt behielt ihren Stolz auch während der spanischen Kolonialherrschaft und gehört als UNESCO-Weltkulturerbe heute zu den wichtigsten und vielfältigsten Stätten Südamerikas. Wer hier, auf 3.300 Metern Höhe und vor einer beeindruckenden Andenkulisse, in die Historie eintauchen möchte, zieht am besten ins Belmond Hotel Monasterio. Aus dem 1592 erbauten Kloster ist das vielleicht schönste bewohnbare Museum in Peru geworden – man lebt hinter altehrwürdigen Mauern, die so dick sind, als müssten sie ihre Gäste vor der Außenwelt schützen, wandelt durch von Rundbögen gesäumte Kreuzgänge und ist beinahe enttäuscht, wenn einem hinter der nächsten Ecke kein Mönch entgegenkommt. Der Grundriss der einstigen Zellen, der Versammlungsräume und der Kapelle wurde kaum verändert – die spartanische Ausstattung aber ist Vergangenheit. Im Belmond Hotel Monasterio gleicht kein Raum dem anderen; hier thront ein plüschiger Sessel, dort prangt ein goldumrahmtes Gemälde; es gibt wertvolle Antiquitäten, blitzblank geputzte Spiegel und Kristallleuchter. Vom Kabelfernsehen bis zur Minibar sind die Zimmer mit allem modernen Komfort ausgestattet und können seit Neuestem sogar mit Sauerstoff angereichert werden, um der unangenehmen Höhenkrankheit vorzubeugen. Nach einer Nacht unter der »Sauerstoffdusche« kann man sich ganz ohne Beschwerden von der Magie Cuzcos verzaubern lassen oder einen Ausflug nach Machu Picchu unternehmen – die »verlorene Stadt der Inka« liegt nur eine dreieinhalbstündige Zugfahrt entfernt.

Buchtipp: »Tod in den Anden« von Mario Vargas Llosa

Suivre les chemins de l'histoire

Lorsque les Incas bâtirent au XVe siècle les premières maisons de Cuzco, ils ne fondèrent pas seulement une capitale – Cuzco était pour eux un lieu sacré et le centre de leur univers. La ville qui garda toute sa fierté même sous la domination des Espagnols, est classée aujourd'hui au patrimoine mondial de l'UNESCO. Elle fait partie des sites les plus importants et les plus pittoresques d'Amérique du Sud. Celui qui désire remonter dans le temps, résidera au Belmond Hotel Monasterio, situé à 3300 mètres d'altitude dans le décor imposant de la cordillère des Andes. Cet ancien monastère datant de 1592 est peut-être le plus beau musée habitable du Pérou. Protégé du monde extérieur par d'épaisses murailles, l'hôte se promène à travers les arcades du cloître et il est presque déçu de ne rencontrer aucun moine au détour de son chemin. Si le plan des cellules, des salles communes et de la chapelle n'a pratiquement pas subi de modifications, l'équipement spartiate fait lui bien partie du passé. Au Belmond Hotel Monasterio, aucune pièce ne ressemble à une autre. Ici trône un fauteuil en peluche, là resplendit le cadre doré d'un tableau. Chaque pièce recèle des antiquités précieuses. Les chambres sont équipées du confort moderne, qui va du câble au minibar, et depuis peu, elles sont même alimentées en oxygène afin d'éviter les effets indésirables de l'altitude. Après une nuit sous la « douche à oxygène » on pourra alors succomber sans problèmes à la magie de Cuzco ou entreprendre une excursion jusqu'au Machu Picchu – la « ville perdue des Incas » n'est en effet qu'à trois-quarts d'heure de train.

Livre à emporter : « Lituma dans les Andes »
de Mario Vargas Llosa

ANREISE	Im Zentrum von Cuzco gelegen, 10 Fahrminuten vom Flughafen entfernt
PREIS	$$$–$$$$
ZIMMER	26 Superior-Zimmer, 78 Deluxe-Zimmer, 15 Junior-Suiten, 4 Präsidenten-Suiten, 2 Royal-Suiten
KÜCHE	2 Restaurants mit peruanischer und internationaler Küche. Am schönsten ist »El Tupay« mit seinem festlichen Inka-Dinner
GESCHICHTE	1592 als Kloster erbaut, seit 1995 ein Hotel
X-FAKTOR	Wo man Historie hautnah erlebt

ACCÈS	Situé dans le centre de Cuzco, 10 min. de l'aéroport
PRIX	$$$–$$$$
CHAMBRES	26 chambres Superior, 78 chambres de luxe, 15 suites junior, 4 suites présidentielles, 2 suites royales
RESTAURATION	2 restaurants proposant une cuisine péruvienne et internationale. Le plus beau est « El Tupay » avec son dîner inca
HISTOIRE	Monastère construit en 1592, hôtel depuis 1995
LES « PLUS »	Un lieu où l'on peut revivre le passé

An unfamiliar way of life...
Kapawi Ecolodge & Reserve, Pastaza

Pictures of paradise...
Hotel San Pedro de Majagua, Islas del Rosario

Bilder vom Paradies

Vor der Küste Kolumbiens fand der französische Maler
Pierre Daguet 1955 sein ganz persönliches Paradies: die Isla
Grande, auf der die Bäume so dicht standen, dass ihre Kro-
nen einen grünen Himmel bildeten, die weiße Sandstrände
besaß und von einem kristallklaren Meer umgeben war, das
bunte Korallenriffe barg. Bei seinen Tauchausflügen in die
Unterwasserwelt scheint Daguet neben exotischen Fischen
auch geheimnisvolle »Ondinas« getroffen zu haben – die
schillernden Nixen jedenfalls verewigte er, zurück an Land,
auf farbenprächtigen Bildern. Heute stehen in seinem ehemaligen Atelier statt der Staffeleien jede Menge Surfbretter
und Segelboote – denn die kleine Hütte ist das Bootshaus
des Hotels San Pedro de Majagua geworden. Zu ihm gehören
17 hübsche Cabanas, die mit ihren naturgedeckten Dächern
so aussehen, als hingen ihnen überlange Ponyfransen ins
Gesicht, und auf deren Terrassen man in gestreiften Hängematten, tiefen Holzsesseln oder auf knallroten Sofas entspannt. Innen sind die Häuschen mit klaren Linien, ausge-
suchten dunklen Möbeln und hellen Stoffen recht puristisch
– doch Accessoires wie eine steinerne Schildkröte auf dem
Boden oder ein orangefarbener Seestern an der Wand setzen
amüsante Akzente. Die Tage ließen sich ohne Weiteres damit
verbringen, über die Insel zu spazieren, auf die glitzernde
See zu schauen und von Daguets Nixen zu träumen ... Doch
man sollte auch an anderer Stelle des Künstlers gedenken,
der nicht nur bunt zeichnen, sondern auch viel trinken konnte: Wenige Meter vom Strand entfernt wurden alle Weinfla-
schen im Meer versenkt, die er in fast 30 Jahren gemeinsam
mit Freunden und bei rauschenden Festen geleert hatte –
inzwischen bilden sie eine Korallenbank, die bei den Einheimischen auch unter dem Namen »Bajo de las Botellas de
Daguet« bekannt ist.
**Buchtipp: »Bericht eines Schiffbrüchigen« von
Garbiel García Márquez**

Images du Paradis

C'est au large de la côte colombienne que le peintre français
Pierre Daguet a trouvé son paradis en 1955 : l'Isla Grande
avec ses arbres si nombreux que leurs couronnes formaient
une voûte de verdure, ses plages de sable blanc, ses eaux cristallines et ses bancs de coraux multicolores. Au cours d'une
de ses plongées sous-marines, Daguet semble avoir rencontré
des poissons exotiques, mais aussi de mystérieuses ondines
qu'il immortalisa sur ses toiles aux couleurs magnifiques.
Aujourd'hui, son ancien atelier ne contient plus de tableaux,
mais une foule de planches à voile et de bateaux car la petite
cabane est devenue l'annexe nautique de l'hôtel San Pedro
de Majagua. Celui-ci comprend 17 jolies « cabanas » qui,
avec leurs toits végétaux, semblent avoir une frange qui leur
tombe sur le visage. Sur leurs terrasses, les hamacs rayés, les
profonds fauteuils en bois et les canapés rouge vif invitent
à la détente. À l'intérieur, les maisonnettes affichent un air
puriste avec leurs meubles sombres aux lignes sobres et
leurs étoffes claires, mais les accessoires comme une tortue
de pierre posée sur le sol ou une étoile orange accrochée au
mur ajoutent une note amusante. On pourrait tout aussi bien
passer ses journées à se promener sur l'île, à regarder les
flots scintillants et à rêver des naïades de Daguet... Pourtant
on peut également rendre un autre hommage à la mémoire
du peintre qui n'aimait pas seulement les couleurs vives,
mais aussi la dive bouteille, en allant voir ce que les habitants
de l'île ont appelé le « Bajo de las Botellas de Daguet » : à
quelques mètres de la plage, on a en effet immergé toutes
les bouteilles de vin que le peintre et ses amis ont bues en
30 ans, au cours de leurs mémorables fêtes. Toutes ces bouteilles forment maintenant une véritable barrière de corail.
**Livre à emporter : « Chronique d'une mort annoncée » de
Gabriel García Márquez**

ANREISE	Auf Isla Grande (Nationalpark Islas del Rosario) gelegen, 45 Bootsminuten südwestlich von Cartagena de Indias
PREIS	$
ZIMMER	4 Cabanas Suites, 10 Cabanas Playa, 3 Cabanas Laguna
KÜCHE	Restaurant mit erstklassigem Seafood
GESCHICHTE	Rings um das ehemalige Atelier von Pierre Daguet gebaut
X-FAKTOR	Für Robinsons Nachfahren und begeisterte Taucher

ACCÈS	Situé sur Isla Grande (parc national Islas del Rosario), à 45 minutes en bateau au sud-ouest de Cartagena de Indias
PRIX	$
CHAMBRES	4 Cabanas Suites, 10 Cabanas Playa, 3 Cabanas Laguna
RESTAURATION	Restaurant proposant des fruits de mer de premier choix
HISTOIRE	Construit autour de l'ancien atelier de Pierre Daguet
LES « PLUS »	Pour les descendants de Robinson Crusoë et les passionnés de plongée

All photos © Tuca Reinés, except

Uxua
pp. 28–37: Mirjam Bleeker,
www.mirjambleeker.nl

Vila Naiá – Paralelo 17°
pp. 70–73, 75–79: Romulo Fialdini, all
photos supplied by the hotel

**Fazenda São Francisco do
Corumbau**
pp. 83–87: all photos supplied
by the hotel

Hotel Santa Teresa
pp. 88–95: all photos supplied
by the hotel

Hotel Fasano Boa Vista
pp. 96–105: all photos supplied
by the hotel

El Garzón
pp. 106–113: Romulo Fialdini,
all photos supplied by the hotel

Casa Zinc Posada
pp. 122–129: Ricardo Labougle,
www.ricardolabougle.com

Yacutinga
pp. 130–131: Yacutinga Lodge/
Carlos Sandoval; p. 135 bottom right:
Yacutinga Lodge/Federico Jacobo;
p. 138: Yacutinga Lodge/Carlos
Sandoval, p. 139: Yacutinga Lodge/
Gustavo Rotta; p. 140 top: Yacutinga
Lodge/Diego Frangi; p. 140 bottom:
Yacutinga Lodge/Diego Frangi;
p. 141 top: Yacutinga Lodge/Federico
Jacobo, p. 141 bottom: Yacutinga
Lodge: Carlos Sandoval

Estancia La Paz
pp. 178–185: all photos supplied by
the hotel

Tipiliuke
pp. 228–229, 234–237: Mirjam Bleeker,
www.mirjambleeker.nl; pp. 230–231,
233: Isaías Miciu

Estancia Arroyo Verde
p. 243 above: © Celine Frers; p. 243
below: © Isaias Miciu; p. 246: supplied
by the hotel

Indigo
pp. 248–253: Mirjam Bleeker,
www.mirjambleeker.nl

Remota
pp. 254–263: Marinella Paolini &
Gianni Franchellucci/Photofoyer,
www.photofoyer.it

explora Patagonia
pp. 264–266, 270–271, 272 below,
273 above: photos supplied by the
hotel

Hotel Antumalal
pp. 274–275, 279 above & below, 280,
282, 283 above & below, 284–285, 286
below, 290–291: Guy Wenborne

explora Atacama
pp. 311 above, 315 below, 318–319:
supplied by the hotel; pp. 312–313,
314 above & below, 315 above,
316–317: Guy Wenborne

Awasi
pp. 320–327: all photos supplied
by the hotel

Kapawi Ecolodge
p. 338, 341 above & below: Diego
Toapanta Garcia/supplied by the hotel

Casa Gangotena
pp. 344–349: all photos supplied
by the hotel

p. 358
Yacutinga Lodge/Photonatura

Photo Credits | Fotonachweis
Crédits photographiques

© 2016 TASCHEN GmbH
Hohenzollernring 53, D-50672 Köln
www.taschen.com

ORIGINAL EDITION:	© 2004 TASCHEN GmbH
© FOR THE WORKS:	Charles and Ray Eames, Venice, CA, www.eamesoffice.com
EDITING AND LAYOUT:	Angelika Taschen, Berlin
TEXT:	Christiane Reiter with contributions by Max Scharnigg
GENERAL PROJECT MANAGER:	Stephanie Bischoff, Cologne
LITHOGRAPH MANAGER:	Thomas Grell, Cologne
ENGLISH TRANSLATION:	Michael Hulse, Warwick; John Sykes, Cologne
FRENCH TRANSLATION:	Thérèse Chatelain-Südkamp, Cologne; Michèle Schreyer, Cologne; Christèle Jany, Cologne
DESIGN:	Lambert und Lambert, Düsseldorf
PRINTED IN	China
ISBN	978-3-8365-5569-2

EACH AND EVERY TASCHEN BOOK PLANTS A SEED!
TASCHEN is a carbon neutral publisher. Each year, we offset our annual carbon emissions with carbon credits at the Instituto Terra, a reforestation program in Minas Gerais, Brazil, founded by Lélia and Sebastião Salgado. To find out more about this ecological partnership, please check: www.taschen.com/zerocarbon
Inspiration: unlimited. Carbon footprint: zero.

To stay informed about TASCHEN and our upcoming titles, please subscribe to our free magazine at www.taschen.com/magazine, follow us on Twitter, Instagram, and Facebook, or e-mail your questions to contact@taschen.com.